THE HOMELESS WEST

AN OVERVIEW

SIMON LENNON

The Homeless West: An Overview
Non-Fiction (Immigration, Race Relations)
A book in the collection: The West
Published by Pine Hill Books
Copyright © 2020 by Simon Lennon.
ISBN 978-1-925446-40-1 (electronic)
ISBN 978-1-925446-41-8 (paperback)
61,000 words
Cover image: London, 2004

In memory of my maternal grandfather

CONTENTS

PREFACE

Uniquely through history and in the world today, white people have opened our borders to other races. We are giving our countries away, accepting of our replacement by others, if not delighting in it. Left vulnerable to other races, we refuse to safeguard each other. Instead, we fight those of our race who defend us.

Examining how we came to this extraordinary situation and its implications is my collection of eleven non-fiction books titled *The West*, comprising four series of two or three books each: *Individualism*, *Identity*, *Nationalism*, and *Cultures*. This overview, *The Homeless West*, collates into a single volume the principal ideas from the third series, *Nationalism*, comprising:

1. *A Land to Belong: Nationalism*.
2. *The Failure of Multiculturalism*.

This overview also includes an appendix, comprising relevant ideas from other books in my collection:

'The Struggle between Races.'

Two companion overviews, *The Unnatural West* and *The Tribeless West*, collate into single volumes the principal ideas from the first two series: *Individualism* and *Identity*. Being unnaturally tribeless, the West is homeless.

These overviews omit the foundations, evidence, and examples supporting those ideas, for which readers so interested may turn to those eleven books and their bibliographies. Generally, those foundations, evidence, and examples are in the book described by the chapter in which those ideas appear. For ease of reading and understanding, some ideas appear in other chapters of this overview and its companion overviews.

Much as the Far East means East Asian races, their cultures, and civilisations and the Middle East means Arabs, Jews, and their cultures and civilisations, so does the West mean peoples racially European, our cultures and civilisation. Whether Europeans are one race or several races and the West is one civilisation or several civilisations, such as English, Welsh, Irish, and so forth, is a matter of nomenclature, as it is for other races and ethnicities. We could be said to be different European races but the same Western Civilisation.

Westerners are white people. People hostile to the West are hostile to white people, and vice versa. People defending one defend the other.

Please consider the ideas in this overview and the books. If the West is going to progress from this Age of Ideology to a New Age of Enlightenment, an Age of Re-Enlightenment, back to reason, morality, and the pursuit of truth, we are going to have to learn again to consider ideas new to us. We will need again to discuss matters rationally with each other.

1. A LAND TO BELONG: NATIONALISM

Like those other races of the world we hold so dear, we of the West carry natures within us. Human nature is to want a home.

Within Europe and elsewhere, European peoples have our private individual rights. We might own some land or some chattels, such as our homes and small beds.

For millennia beforehand, we also believed, as other races still believe, in collective interests, rights, and ownership. People shared possessions with their families and sometimes their clans and religious brethren because they were families, clans, and religious brethren.

It is a notion we recall when we speak of the family home, even if too few of us still think of the family possessing it. We are more likely to think that merely the parents possess it, or that only one of the parents possesses it.

Some possessions people held because we shared possession with the rest of our nations and races. Most importantly and profoundly, we owned our countries: our collective homes.

Families share homes much better than homes that family members could afford living alone. Races share land much greater than land each family owns.

Our forebears built and defended our countries to their deaths, before bequeathing them to us. They presumed we too would build upon and defend our countries, before bequeathing them to our shared descendants.

In much the same way, other races' forebears left lands and homes for them. Some lands their forebears conquered on their collective behalf.

Nomadic tribes moved around because they needed to move around for food and water. Their homes might have been their tents, but they were homes nevertheless. Their homelands were the hills, plains, or sands they roamed, distinct from the hills, plains, or sands that other tribes roamed.

Gypsy homes are often still caravans, commanding parks, farms, and other land, if only for a time. Gypsies need to move around.

Other people make their homes longer lasting. When circumstances allow it, their homes are homelands.

African tribes mark out their tribal lands, if only by the rivers and mountains. Arab tribes stake out their sands and emirates, if only by the space from others. Islanders know which islands are theirs off other people's coasts and in the long-lost South Pacific.

Other races but ours keep their inherited lands in their racial and other tribal hands, even their family hands. Fa'a Samoa includes keeping island land in Samoan family hands.

They defend their homes and lands if need be, or try to defend them, often expanding them if they can, to bequeath to their descendants. They do so in honour of their forebears, for the sake of their descendants, and for them and their compatriots.

Only the West gives our lands away. Without racism, we no longer care for the legacy of our forebears or lives of our descendants. Without nationalism, we no longer care about our compatriots, who no longer care about us.

Patriotism, Nationalism

"Patriotism is the last refuge of a scoundrel," said Englishman Samuel Johnson in 1775. Today, we quote Johnson's words to criticise patriotism, but he intended his words to criticise scoundrels, knowing how generous of heart patriots are.

Patriotism is a love for one's country. With patriotism comes loves for one's compatriots and cultures.

Some people contrast patriotism with nationalism to suggest that nationalism is more of a willingness to harm other countries. It is not. If nationalism lacks the emotion of patriotism, it is because nationalism lacks emotion altogether.

Nationalism is more a matter of reason and practicality than emotion. It is recognition that nation states, sovereign and distinct, are in people's best interests, safeguarding people, races, and cultures.

To that end, nationalism encompasses co-operation among compatriots sharing a collective national identity, knowing such co-operation to be in all of their interests. Love is patriotism. Loyalty is nationalism.

As well as possessing our private dwellings, be they rural estates or one-bedroom sitters above old shops, nationalism means people possessing a country: a homeland of our own. It is possession shared among a race or other tribe sharing a common collective identity. To possess a country, people need not possess private property, not even that sitter in which we reside for as long as we can scramble together the money to pay rent.

Without nationalism, we no longer feel the lands we inherited or even Europe are collectively ours. We are losing our lands to belong. We became the homeless West.

The Peace of Nationalism

As a process, nationalism was the bringing together of disparate city-states and other states of the same race and religion, with their palaces, villages, and cottages, into cohesive entities: nations. Nationalism grew from a need for peace and security, especially through nineteenth-century Europe. Liberation from the French and Austrians were among the motives gradually melding Italian states into Italy.

Napoleon Bonaparte and other French military threats motivated Germanic states to confederate in 1814 and the Protestant Germanic states eventually to unify in 1871, the latter without Roman Catholic Austria for the efforts of Otto von Bismarck. Before nationalism united them, Prussian and other Germanic soldiers arguably had more to fear from their officers than from their battlefield enemies.

Feeling a common identity, nationalists were concerned for their compatriots. Soldiers had often been mercenaries fighting for plunder before nationalism gave them reason to defend their people: their men, women, and children. Nationalism was virtuous.

As was often the case, the calamitous Great War changed everything. Without the Great War, nationalism would still be virtuous.

Germany not having unified until 1871 and with Bismarck reluctant to build an empire, Germany's empire was much smaller than other empires by the time of the Great War. Instead of breaking up after the Great War, Germany's scattered small empire became parts of the great British Empire.

While the Great War brought down the Russian, Austro–Hungarian, and Ottoman empires, it facilitated nationalism among races and ethnic groups previously denied their nations by those empires. Many of those races and ethnic groups were European.

The Russian Empire dissolved in 1918. From that breakdown arose the republics of Russia, Belarus, Ukraine, and Transcaucasia, although the multiracial, multi-religious Transcaucasia lasted only a short time before separating into Armenia, Georgia, and Azerbaijan in April 1918.

Nationalism is natural. Multiracial superstates are not. They depend upon monetary, military, or other force to hold them together.

Blaming Nationalism

The desire for peace that drove nationalism in the nineteenth century as a matter of reason became, for white people, a force against nationalism in the twentieth century as a matter of emotion. We think our national interests mean not having nations, believing nations led us to war.

We blame the Great War on nationalism for inspiring our leaders to embark upon war, but that was militarism. We fear nationalism dragging us to kill and be killed, but the problem was not the patriotism of our men marching off to war. It was the lack of patriotism among our leaders creating and continuing the carnage, condemning our good men to fight and to die.

The same could be said of World War II for Britain and Germany. It could be said of many wars for many countries.

When Britain allied with the communist Soviet Union after its invasion by Germany in June 1941, we did not just fight Germany together, eventually destroying Germany and German nationalism. We empowered those who would erase our races, countries, and cultures too.

We weakened nationalism across the West. We slowly surrendered our resolve to defend our races, countries, and cultures again.

Nationalism fell into disrepute, so far as the West is concerned, because our nations fell into disrepute. Other nations did not fall into disrepute, for us or for them.

Jewish nationalism treats German and other white people's nationalism as synonymous with fascism, bundling genocide into the nationalistic wrong because Jews bundle everything about Nazism with genocide. We have come to do the same. Doing so does not fairly or accurately treat nationalism, or fascism.

In 1939, when World War II began, Western countries were communist (the Soviet Union), fascist (Germany, Hungary, Italy, Spain, and Portugal), or nationalist democracies. Most were nationalist democracies. By melding nationalism with fascism, we lost our scope for liberal nationalism: democratic racism.

German Nationalism

We blame World War II on nationalism because we blame the war on Nazis and Nazis were so demonstrative with their nationalism, but to deny Germany her nationalism is to deny Germans their self-determination. Bringing ethnic Germans and the territory they occupied from neighbouring countries into the Reich was a feature of Germany's aggression up to World War II.

Bringing Germanic Austria into Germany had been discussed by Austrians and Germans alike ever since Germany's formation without Austria in 1871. Germany and Austria might have united after the Great War, but the Allied powers prohibited any Anschluss in the 1919 Treaty of Versailles. Denying Germans and Austrians their self-determination was more of the cruel injustice imposed upon them at Versailles.

In 1938, Austrian troops did not resist the German invasion. Austrians overwhelmingly ratified the Anschluss in a plebiscite soon afterwards.

Other German aggression was not due simply to German nationalism. It was a consequence of the failure of trying to bring different ethnic groups into other countries, even when those ethnic groups are of the same broad race.

The Sudetenland was ethnically German and part of Austria–Hungary until her collapse during the Great War. With the dissolution of Austria–Hungary, those ethnic Germans wanted to join Germany, but Czechs forced those German areas into their new country, Czechoslovakia. Subsequently imposing the Czech language on German schools added to ethnic German grievances, as did other Czech actions against ethnic Germans. They thus added to German support for German dictator Adolf Hitler bringing the Sudetenland into Germany in 1938.

Czechs regarded the Munich Agreement of 1938, recognising Hitler's actions in the Sudetenland, as a betrayal by Britain and France. Ethnic Germans in the Sudetenland saw the Agreement as their self-determination the Czechs had denied them for twenty years.

Germany subsequently absorbing the Czech areas of Czechoslovakia in 1939 had no such rationale, but it was also imposing upon Czechs what Czechs had imposed upon Germans in the Sudetenland through those preceding twenty years. It was, essentially, revenge.

Also keen to take their opportunity to escape the Czechs, Slovakia declared her independence from Czechoslovakia. With no sense of revenge against Slovaks as there might have been against Czechs, Germany respected Slovakian independence. Slovakia became Germany's ally.

Denying Germans their nationalism is also denying Germans their right to redress wrongs they suffered as a nation, most pointedly at Versailles in 1919. Nationalism is justice.

The Treaty of Versailles also stripped land from Germany to give to Poland. It created the Polish Corridor, separating most of Germany from East Prussia and the city of Danzig.

From its inception, the Polish Corridor caused massive resentment across Germany. No Weimar government recognised it.

Through the 1920s and '30s, Polish policies and other forces drove an exodus of Germans from the Polish Corridor, replacing them with Poles. They made the will of the local people irrelevant by replacing the local people.

There is a view that in 1939 Hitler ordered the annexation of the Czech areas of Czechoslovakia before the invasion of Poland because he saw Germany's claim to those Czech areas as being weak, unlike Germany's claim to the Polish Corridor. He reasoned, wrongly, that Britain would not deny Germany recovering land that the 1919 Treaty of Versailles had cruelly taken from Germany to give to Poland.

Poland had only come back into being because of the Great War. At the start of September 1939, Nazi Germany was simply the latest country through the centuries to invade her. Germany was not the last.

Self-Determination

Having lost confidence in ourselves after two world wars and the Holocaust, the West clamoured for something other than our race, countries, and cultures in which to believe. We found it in everyone else: their races, countries, and cultures.

The victors of World War II created the United Nations. Adopted in June 1945, the month after World War II finished in Europe and while the war remained under way in Asia and the Pacific, the Charter of the United Nations declared the Purposes of the United Nations to be: *"To develop friendly relations among nations based on respect for the principle of equal rights and self-determination of peoples..."*

Self-determination of peoples is nationalism. Relations among nations are internationalism. Nationalism is not a matter of superiority, but equality.

With the Jewish Holocaust in mind, our focus then was on other races' self-determination. We failed then to appreciate how much we would come to need to rediscover notions of nationalism for us.

Self-determination for races is racism. We object to white people's nationalism because we object to white people's racism, and vice versa.

Respecting rights for other races, left to their countries and choices, we slowly lost notions of nation for us. Our view of institutions like the United Nations progressed from being a means of nations interrelating with each other to structures superseding nations altogether.

Other races and countries saw their opportunities. The United Nations and other global bodies became more means for them to assert their national interests over us.

While countries outside the West select whatever international rules and edicts suit their national interests, we submit to the dictates of the United Nations and other international bodies, along with their assemblies of bureaucrats, without thought of our national interests. Defending our national interests would be nationalism. Even recognising that we have national interests would be nationalism.

In the absence of global elections, we interpret the world's will and interests. The West became our laboratory for a single world civilisation. From 1992, the European Union became our model.

Britons voted in 2016 to leave the European Union above all else for a homeland again. Those most in favour were those who remembered a British homeland being happy, safe, and secure. From their roughest of local council accommodations to the greenest of pastures at the far side of the world, we wanted our collective home again.

We were not harking back to the days of Empire, glorious as those days were, as critics accused us of doing. We simply wanted our country back. We wanted Britain back.

Many of the people who voted in favour of remaining in the European Union respected the result. Many did not. It seemed the relentless opponents of respecting that referendum result through the ensuing years did so because of their contempt for Britain, especially but not only England, contempt for Britons, and contempt for the West.

Globalism

In ancient times, Jewish nationalist revolutions against the Roman Empire beginning in 66 A.D. became known as the Jewish-Roman War or Wars. Jewish losses, especially the fall of Jerusalem and destruction of the Second Temple in 70 A.D., scattered the Jews. They became the first global people.

Jews retained their nationalism. They simply lacked a national land in their hands: a homeland they possessed.

Being a global people did not make Jews globalists. The ideology of globalism sees or seeks a world without nations: without races or other peoples; without national borders. It is a rejection of nationalism.

Among the scattered Jews of the nineteenth century, living without a land of his own, was Karl Marx. He devised the first of the globalist ideologies: communism. In place of national collectivism among people of the same race sharing their country, communism envisaged a global collectivism: people of more than one race sharing a country or several countries, and eventually people of all races sharing the world.

The communist Soviet Union formed in 1922. Fundamental to the failure of the Soviet Union and its eventual dissolution in 1991 was its pursuit of a superstate denying peoples their races and nations.

Marxists dismiss the comprehensive failures of communism by claiming those countries that thought they were communist were not really communist, although at the time communists the world over also thought those countries were communist. Only after those countries failed did communists everywhere decide those countries had not really been communist.

In particular, Marxists now insist that communism must be global, encompassing all the lands and people on earth: a single world superstate erasing all national borders. Ipso facto, because communism has not been completely global, there cannot have been any communist countries.

There is no logical reason why Marxist political and economic theory depends upon communism covering the earth in a single world state, in spite of Marx's presumption that communism eventually would. There is only the brutal reality that countries not subject to communism point to the failures of countries subject to communism.

Another ideological globalism unfolded across the ruptured West after World War II: individualism. We surrendered our senses of belonging because, following the Holocaust, we did not want anything separating us from the Jews. Our countries became homes for Jews as much as for us, although for the most part, they had been for centuries.

Western countries slowly became homes for everyone. Becoming homes for everyone, Western countries became homes for no one.

Communism having failed, the remaining globalists are typically individualists, caring only for themselves and their sense of their individual selves. Global collectivism depends upon every race coming aboard, giving up their countries into the mix. Individualism the West can do alone, giving up our countries for nothing in return.

The multiculturalist West dreams of a world without nations, but our globalism is the globalism of everyone else. When we give up our countries, we do not gain the world. We just lose our countries.

Globalisation

With our single world view, without race and thus without collective culture, we of the West are citizens of the world. The rest of the world does not recognise the concept.

Globalisation is not globalism. Globalisation presumes races and nations.

Globalisation is countries trading and otherwise engaging with each other, bettering their peoples behind their borders and their peoples beyond their borders. Citizens are aware of what is happening elsewhere while, for the most part, leaving each other be.

Most countries outside the West have opened windows to the world. All of them retain their walls. Openness is for their peoples, not everyone else.

Theirs are territories distinct and, to the extent they can make them, inviolable, with the comfort countries are and all that countries give them. Their lands are theirs, not anyone else's.

They have homelands. They have homes.

Foreigners can visit their countries and perhaps stay for a while, even a long while or to the end of their lives, if those countries have no reason to reject them. Foreigners have not so much rights to reside as permission to stay. Those countries revoke that permission if their people's interests require it. Only some countries offer citizenship, and those countries only to their race, religion, or small specific categories of resident applicant or individuals. None let foreigners vote.

Racially homogenous countries are not closed societies. They are simply societies, serving people within them rather than people wanting to enter.

When countries outside the West allow people to visit, it is in their national interests. Those countries might be impoverished but want money. They might be wealthy and see value in the work foreigners do that their people cannot do, or will not do.

Foreigners leave when their work is done.

Those countries allow tourists and workers within their borders, without imagining foreigners are anything but foreigners. Laws in the interests of local people are not being changed to accommodate others. Theirs is a right to defend their kin and themselves: expelling those who would harm their countries, cultures, and compatriots.

Globalisation does not require immigration. Tourism, employment, and aid do not require immigration. A multiracial world does not require multiracial countries.

White Individualism

Being a citizen of the world once meant our Western sense of seeing and acting worldwide, while being loyal citizens of our city-states and countries: our races. That thinking underpinned Western and other imperialism.

Without racism or nationalism, we have come to interpret being a citizen of the world as being worldwide, without loyalty to our race or nation. We think that makes us part of the planet, but it makes us part of no place at all.

A word we use to describe the West unilaterally opening our borders to all is globalisation, but it is not globalisation. It is individualism.

We give our countries to strangers as if our countries were only ours to give, without sense that we share our countries with our forebears, compatriots, and descendants. Had it not been for Western individualism, there would have been no interracial immigration, certainly not to any significant degree. There would be no multiculturalism.

For all our rights in our individualist West, a rare right we do not have is a right to a country. A country is a people with territory, but we are no longer peoples. We might be the smallest of minorities or, for the time being at least, the majority, but our nations are not changing because we feel we have no nations to change.

Our only rights to land (and everything else) are as individuals. We might own pockets of soil, if that, or spaces of air. Outside the West, we do not even have that.

Without nations of our own, we imagine belonging with others. We do not.

No other races concede what we are conceding. Without homelands of our own, we can spend forever pursuing a place in which to belong, never finding it among other races.

White Nationalism

Having suffered the loss of their countries and cultures to communism, East Europeans recovered their countries and cultures after communism collapsed from 1989 through to the dissolution of the Soviet Union in 1991. They now defend their races, countries, and civilisation, as the rest of the West no longer defends ours.

In 1916, Irish nationalism united capitalists, socialists, workers, and poets, lauding Irish people and cultures. The Proclamation of the Irish Republic declared *"the right of the people of Ireland to the ownership of Ireland and to the unfettered control of Irish destinies, to be sovereign and indefeasible."*

A century later, Irish nationalism still longs to wrestle Ulster from the United Kingdom. It now does so only to give her with the rest of Ireland to the European Union.

So-called Scottish independence is the same. Scottish nationalism no longer loves Scotland. It simply hates England.

Genuine nationalists would not submerge their countries in the European Union or any other globalist superstate. They do not want mass immigration.

For the most part, nationalism early in the twenty-first century no longer means people gaining their nations. Nationalism has come to mean people retaining their nations: their homelands and self-determination.

What came to be called white nationalism is white people defending our particular race, culture, and civilisation or defending white people and Western cultures and civilisation generally, even from mere abuse. Immigrants condemn white nationalism because white nationalism would resist their imperialism: their races coming and growing in our countries, asserting their cultures and other interests at the expense of ours.

We are the only race on earth condemning imperialism by our

own. We are the only race on earth condemning nationalism by our own.

Western nationalism disgusts us. Other people's nationalism does not.

Other races do not need to talk of their nationalism. Races that have not opened their borders to other races are not so vulnerable to other races assailing theirs. They have no need to defend their countries and cultures when nobody threatens their countries and cultures, and when their corporations and compatriots already defend them. Their governments are not giving up their countries, cultures, and races, as our governments and we are giving up ours.

Nobody minds races other than ours defending their countries, cultures, and races. For the most part, nobody worries about other races' nationalism.

While other races' nationalism remains unmentioned, people talk of white nationalism because immigration commands white people who care for our races, countries, and cultures to speak up. White people's nationalism is akin to other races' nationalism, so that condemning white people's nationalism without also condemning other races' nationalism is condemning white people.

The Fractured West

Away from Eastern Europe, in control are the globalists, the multiculturalists: neglectful and often belligerent towards Western countries, cultures, and races. Normally hiding from public shaming and punishment, or simply too weak, tired, or uncertain of themselves to resist, are Western nationalists: caring for our countries, cultures, and races.

Other races side with whoever suits them. They defend and advance their races by supporting multiculturalism and other diversity for the West when their races benefit from it but not when their races suffer from it, as their races can suffer when other races hostile to them benefit too much.

In the homeless West, multiculturalism has become an all-pervasive ideology erasing everything rational, natural, and just in its path. Western ideals aiming to better people's lives that once were nationalist and racist have slowly become multiculturalist, including socialism, capitalism, conservatism, and liberalism. They no longer better our lives.

What had been competing ideas for advancing civilisation became ideological, uninterested in Western countries and cultures, if not hostile towards them. In such an environment, any traditional white socialist, capitalist, conservative, liberal, or anything else willing to defend Western Civilisation, cultures, and races became selfish, evil, and odd.

The conflict between nationalism and multiculturalism is a uniquely Western conflict: an internecine clash between those who value the West and Western cultures (as people of other races remain free to value their races and cultures) and those who do not. It is the tussle between support and separation, self-belief and self-loathing, self-determination and self-destruction. It is the struggle between nature and ideology, between fact and fabrication, between reason and emotion, but the emotion not of love but of hate. It is the battle between trying to move on from the Holocaust and remaining in the mire.

Moving on from the Holocaust does not mean forgetting the Holocaust, because we should not forget anything. It means remembering not just the Holocaust but also everything else.

We should learn from the past, but not remain there. Only then can we confront the reality of the present and risks of the future.

Selective Diversity

There can hardly be a more ubiquitous chant around the homeless West than our chant of diversity in demonic unison at every opportunity. Underpinning our talk of diversity is diversity of race.

Unable to bear hearing that word, we speak of cultural diversity or simply diversity. We really mean racial diversity.

Ours is not a culture of diversity. We welcome only certain diversities. Diversity does not extend to the politics and principles that have become our identity, in this Age of Ideology.

There is no diversity when it comes to white people's views about race. Celebrating racial diversity is no more or less an acknowledgment of race than would be celebrating our dwindling areas of racial homogeneity but, instead of being merely a matter of nature or taste, we demand diversity while being hostile to any hint of white homogeneity. We do not want white people's racism.

Preferring a multiracial populace means we believe our countries are better than they used to be for no other reason than accommodating other races, our cities better for their races no longer being ours. Whether we are among a dozen or a dozen million people, we would rather be around other races than around only ours. For two of us to be diversity, then we deliberately desire the other person to be from another race. If he or she is not, then we must wish we were.

Diversity is not about other races. It is about us.

We are not celebrating other races when we celebrate diversity. We are celebrating our individual selves: that we are not racist.

Adopting for our individual selves the mantras of moral superiority, every foreign face to which we smile, foreign hand we shake, generosity to foreign lives we bestow, is our gloating that we have come to be so great. We pat each other on our backs and kiss each other fondly for not being the people we once were.

We think we have advanced not just above other white people inferior to us (with their racist failings we merrily deride) but also above other races with their racist flaws: their racial homogeneity. We think that makes us better than they are, not collectively (for that would be racist) but individually. We claim to lead the world, but will still insist that we do not.

All we celebrate about us is our new-found conviction that white people are no better than others, but by refusing to espouse diversity for other races' countries, clubs, and communities, we are calling our race worse. We beg countries outside the West to tolerate minority races already present, just as we do, but for all our lauding of diversity as our supposed strength, we do not expect countries outside the West to allow interracial immigration. Thinking that countries without us would be better for our immigration was the thinking behind European colonialism.

We do not think that anymore. We do not even insist that other countries would be better for other immigration.

Instead, we prefer a European and non-European to two Europeans but not to two non-Europeans. We do not like our race at all.

Celebrating diversity is more than merely indifference to white people. It is hostility towards us.

Multiculturalism

Referring to culture when we mean race is among the West's new secrets of language. When culture sounds too much, we reduce it to cultural background. Multiculturalism is another euphemism for multiracialism.

Multiculturalism is also our most optimistic perspective of racial diversity. It imagines social cohesion developing amidst racial difference.

Central to multiculturalism is a contradiction. While we cannot find common threads with our forebears, compatriots, or descendants, we are supposed to feel common threads with the rest of the world.

The rest of the world feels no such commonality. Other races retain their common threads with their forebears, compatriots, or descendants: their races and nations, not ours or anyone else's.

There is no multicultural "we." There is only multiculturalism.

Nationalism allows "we." So does racism.

We presume immigration and multiculturalism are the norm around the world. They are not, but we are not wondering why other races hang onto their birth rights: their racial and other tribal homes. We are not even noticing.

Nationalists and racists look around. Individualists are self-absorbed.

We might talk of the narrowness of nationalism, but when we abandoned our empires and opened our nations to all races, we became oblivious to everyone else. We see immigrant faces in our country, feel they flatter us by coming, and believe they are like us.

So self-centric have we become, we do not think much beyond our close social boundaries: the people we know, the people we meet. We think little of the suburbs and cities in which we live, beyond those streets we see every day. We think even less of the far side of the world. Ours is a one-world ideology, without regard to the rest of the world.

Advancing multiculturalism for the West but not elsewhere, we advance other races at our races' expense. Defending multiculturalism, we defend other races from ours.

Other People's Empires

While we lament that the lands on which we built our empires we supposedly stole from native tribes, those native tribes stole those same lands from each other. Tribes fought bloody battles with each other for as long as anybody knew, and long before ever seeing a white man or woman's face.

Neither was building empires across racial lines ever unique to Europeans. Other races fought, conquered, and ruled each other and us, with their empires and aspiring empires. Conquerors killed and pillaged without thought of bettering the lives of local people. Some killed and pillaged without thought of anything but killing and pillaging.

In the year 492 B.C. and again in 480 B.C., Persia invaded Greece, massacring every remaining Athenian and destroying much of Athens, including the Acropolis, in 480 and 479 B.C. In 479 B.C., the Athenian, Spartan, and other Greek city states defeated the Persians. They went onto expel the Persians from Europe altogether. Thus ancient Greece survived, headed into its golden age.

City-states and nations do not simply defend us and our lifestyles. They allow us to flourish.

North African Arabs, Berbers, and Muladi conquered and colonised the Iberian Peninsula from 711, submitting Spaniards and Portuguese to a series of Muslim caliphates and dhimmi. Romanticising other races as we now do, today we call it multiculturalism. Our forebears did not. Spaniards and Portuguese finally expelled the last of the Moorish invaders in 1502.

Mongols remain proud of Genghis Khan, who founded the Mongol Empire of the thirteenth and fourteenth centuries. Historians estimate that the Mongol invasions across Asia and into Eastern Europe killed forty million people, amounting to about ten percent of the world's population, and perhaps as many as sixty million people.

Their murders were arguably genocides, at least of the Tangut in 1227. Also arguably genocide and if so then the most geographically widespread genocide in history, the Mongol Empire encouraged mixed-race marriage and thus mixed-race child bearing across the lands it conquered.

Nor did our forebears romanticise bloody Turkish conquests

and colonisation, which occupied much of Southern and Eastern Europe for centuries and reached the Gates of Vienna in 1529 and then again in 1683. Turks have never been expelled from Anatolia.

Longer lasting than later British rule over India was rule over India by the Mughal Empire. That empire is unknown to us today.

We do not condemn other people's empires as we now condemn our own. We admire other races and their forebears for exploration and empires we condemn by our race and forebears. We do not take offence from African, Asian, and other races' imperialism as we take it from past European imperialism.

European Empires

When an empire reached far enough, imperialism became globalisation, not globalism. European imperialism was predicated upon nations: upon races enjoying homelands albeit under our control, if necessary or desirable.

European imperialism had spread civilisation since Alexander the Great conquered the Persian Empire. Tutored by the philosopher Aristotle in his youth and taking books with him wherever he travelled and fought, Alexander brought Greek culture, including philosophy and styles of cities, to Asia and North Africa. He also drew upon all that he considered worthwhile from other civilisations to develop what was arguably the first world civilisation: Hellenistic Civilisation. He died aged thirty-two, in 323 B.C.

More recent European colonialism also followed us evicting foreign colonisers from Europe. Portuguese and Spaniards launched the Age of Discovery in the fifteenth century while progressively rolling back North African colonisation of their homelands.

Throughout our age of European imperialism, we did not colonise countries with something like civilisation securely and peacefully in place, such as Siam and Tonga. They both became nation states with modern freedoms and laws in response to approaching European empires.

Unlike other races, Europeans explored the world and conquered much of it with the best of intentions. European colonial powers built wonderfully impressive empires with thought of helping not just ourselves but also local populations. Most times and places we did.

Internecine violence in India was so severe and widespread during the nineteenth century that the Indian population was reputedly falling until the East India Company and then the British Crown and Empire brought order. The British Empire built railroads connecting warring tribes and warlords, facilitating Indian nationalism. With nationalism, came peace.

Knowing Western Civilisation to be civilisation, we shared civilisation with the world: fostering arts, culture, government, and society. Where there previously were none, we crafted states, introducing civil service and public administration for everyone's benefit. We built roads, schools, and hospitals.

We stood tall among races. We made some mistakes, but still made the world better.

Amidst the general hostility to white people, there are those who now accuse us of profiting from our empires. In fact, the British Empire was expensive for Britain and British people to develop, defend, and administer. Any returns on the investments we made were less than returns we could have made upon investments at home, but we invested around the empire because we wanted to better the world. Other Europeans did too. Simple pillaging, as conquerors from other races undertook, would have made more financial sense.

Christian missionaries in particular aided education, democratic freedoms, and economic development, continuing long after they had left. When we are not encouraging other races to hate us, they do not think our empires were bad.

European empires kept African tribes from killing each other. The conflicts we controlled through our era of empire resumed when we departed.

To imagine most races of the world building without us what we built for them is ludicrous. Unwilling to distinguish one race from another, at least to our advantage, we imagine it anyway.

We long ago withdrew from most of the countries we colonised, leaving behind the structures of civilisation still used there: public buildings, roads and railways, water systems and farming. Away from the most devoted of government patronage or tourist incomes and without the benefit of our administration, other vestiges of empire greyed. The heritage is not theirs to preserve.

Defaming the Dead

We talk of the benefits to other European countries of Roman and Napoleonic invasions. Having lost our self-belief and been convinced by others of Western wickedness, we refuse to acknowledge the benefits to other races from Europe's grand age of global empire.

The best thing that happened to this planet was the British Empire. The worst was multiculturalism, but while we cast no blame upon immigrants into the West for the ills they bring with them, we are not so forgiving of our forebears.

Nobody blames Asia for the Black Death from 1346 to 1353, which killed more than a quarter and perhaps half the population of Europe, as many as fifty million Europeans. The plague's origins are unclear, but it probably originated in the Mongol sieges of the Genoese port of Caffa in Crimea through the 1340s. In 1346, Mongols catapulted the bodies of their plague-infected soldiers over the city walls. Genoese fled, probably bringing the plague to Europe in rats aboard merchant ships.

Accusing immigrants today of spreading disease, committing crimes, and obliterating our cultures would be racist. Conversely, suggesting our imperialist forebears did anything else but spread disease, commit crimes, and obliterate our cultures is racist.

While conducting programmes trying to reduce disease among our dominions, colonial Europeans sometimes unwittingly spread disease, but we care little what our forebears reasoned. We do not care that they came without meaning to harm. We deride them for thinking they could do any good.

Germany's Holocaust Law prohibits Germans from defaming the dead. Germany imprisons Germans who supposedly defame dead Jews by claiming the Holocaust *did not* occur, although the reason such denial defames dead Jews is not clear.

Conversely, we defame our dead. We claim genocides of indigenous peoples by colonial Europeans *did* occur.

If we wanted to carry out genocide of indigenous tribes and races, then we would have carried it out. Indigenous tribes and races survived because we did not want to kill them, beyond what conquest and the defence of our race required. We wanted to help them.

They sometimes killed us. We sometimes killed them. They often killed each other.

Much as Australian Aborigines killed each other, British settlers and Aborigines killed each other in conflicts over food, livestock, and water. Where the killing of Aborigines appeared unlawful, British courts tried the white settlers responsible. Talk of a Tasmanian genocide was a lie.

In the Americas, indigenous tribes and races fought each other, killed each other, and stole each other's land. They could be as brutal with their tribespeople as with other tribespeople.

No worse than they were, the most aggressive European builders of empire were the Spaniards and Portuguese, but the Iberians had suffered almost eight centuries of occupation at home under Muslim Moorish caliphates. North Africans invaders had made them familiar with intercontinental conquest.

Building Countries

Immigrants are not generic. They were not simply immigrants but British and Irish who built Australia and New Zealand. French built Quebec and Louisiana. British and Irish built the rest of Canada. British, Irish, Germans, and other North Europeans built America. Portuguese built Brazil. Spanish built the rest of Latin America. Other Europeans contributed to most countries, depending upon colonial powers employing or allowing them.

The contributions from other races to building our countries were tiny, if anything. Those that came often worked, fairly earning money for themselves, but only our new-found determination to embrace them and to diminish our forebears lets us think they contributed materially to building our countries.

Europeans built countries in and away from Europe, before and after other races came. We contributed to countries we did not build.

Talk of America being a melting pot began by the 1780s, although it became most popularised by a play of that name first staged in 1908. Today, we imagine that to be a melting pot of the world, but America was a North European melting pot, especially of English and Germans. The 1908 play by a Russian Jewish immigrant may well have reflected the playwright's global ambitions, but the popular interpretation of the phrase remained one of North Europeans.

Latin American colonies were Spanish or Portuguese, in spite of their English and other European enclaves. If they were melting pots, they were Southern Europe's melting pots, even while countries like Argentina enjoyed English immigrants too.

Other colonies were not melting pots. In spite of their Irish, German, and other European enclaves, Australia, New Zealand, and Canada aside from Quebec were British. Quebec was French. Canada was no melting pot but two distinct and separate ethnic groups and cultures, which might be called races and civilisations: British and French.

If the British colonies were melting pots, it was because being British could be a melting pot: of English, Scottish, Welsh, and for some of us Irish. Being British could also mean remaining English, Scottish, Welsh, or sometimes through history Irish, co-operating with our fellow Britons.

When being Irish was pointedly not being British, Ireland was no melting pot. We could be cruel to each other as we never were to other races.

The End of Empires

If the Age of European Empires did not end with the end of World War II, it ended with the start of World War II. That was the war not in Europe but in Asia.

The Japanese Empire dated from 1868, with the Japanese people increasingly pressing their leaders to assert their country's presence overseas. Korea came within the Japanese sphere of influence with the Japan–Korea Treaty of 1876, became a protectorate of Japan in 1905, and came under Japanese occupation with Japan's annexation of Korea in 1910.

The first Sino–Japanese War led to the Treaty of Shimonoseki in 1895, by which China ceded Taiwan, the Pescadores Islands, and the Liaodong Peninsula (southern Manchuria) to Japan. It also forced China to open its ports of Chongqing, Hangzhou, Shashi, and Suzhou to Japanese trade.

Seeing Russia as a threat to its imperial ambitions, Japan started the Russo–Japanese War with a surprise attack in 1904. Ultimata and declarations of war are European etiquette. Other races make surprise attacks.

Russia's defeat by Japan was a European country's worst defeat by an Asian country in centuries. It inspired the first Russian Revolution in 1905, which Lenin later called a dress rehearsal for the communist revolution in 1917.

Russia's defeat also diminished the threat that Germany and Austria–Hungary felt from Russia in 1914. Thus it contributed to Austria–Hungary's ultimatum against Russia's ally Serbia, which precipitated the Great War.

The Russo–Japanese War essentially set boundaries between the Russian and Japanese Empires, without rolling back the Russian Empire. That would happen with the Great War.

Japan's presence in China expanded with its conquest of Manchuria in 1931 and the rest of China in 1937, in which Japan attacked European interests also stationed in China. With Europeans consumed with World War II in Europe, Japan attacked our empires and America, brutally spreading across Asia and the Pacific Ocean. Eating into European Empires, Japan most infamously captured citadel Singapore from the British Empire in 1942.

America, Britain, and our allies ended the Japanese Empire in 1945. We recovered Singapore and our other lands of Empire and liberated other territories from Japan, but without the will to be again what we had been.

Weakened by a second world war and without faith anymore in the civilisation we once spread, the age of European Empires also ended. Where once we entered other races' homelands, we withdrew, coming home to Europe, America, and Australasia. The United Nations called it decolonisation, removing Europeans from most of Africa, Asia, and the Pacific, but not Asians from Africa or the Pacific.

Tribes and races across Asia, Africa, and the oceans became again nations they had once been. They became independent countries they had never before been.

Something else happened, because our end of empires was not about empires. It was about us.

Race and Country

Countries are all premised upon race and racism, right across the world. It only bothers us that Western countries used to be.

Broken by two world wars and a holocaust, we lost our senses of race. We soon lost our senses of home.

One explanation as to why Britain and France opened our borders to our former colonial possessions in numbers we had never previously imagined was gratitude to soldiers who had helped defend us during World War II, but any gratitude was not limited to those who fought. Besides, thousands of Indians had volunteered for the German Army's *Legion Freies Indien* and the Italian Army fighting against us, including some prisoners of war who had formerly fought with us. We still admitted Indians.

We also allowed other races, with no participation in the war, to come. Western countries with no history of empire or participation in the war unilaterally opened their borders too.

Without racism, we lost our resolve to occupy not only other people's lands, but our lands too. Interracial immigration, especially in significant numbers, depends upon the decline of our racial identities.

Nations make little sense without race. Nationalism makes little sense without racism. Geographical delineations make little sense without biological delineations.

Nationalism depends on racism. Without being a people, we cannot be a country.

A race can comprise many nations. A nation comprises only one race. Any other races living within national borders submit to the dominant race, except in the West.

Countries segregate races behind borders, if those borders are enforced. Our rejection of race is our rejection of country, no matter how many other races are among our citizenry. Anything else would be discriminatory.

Countries discriminate if they offer something more, however trivial, to their citizens than to others. Such a frenzy do we have around discrimination, discrimination against foreigners we meet with abuse, even if the discrimination is not to their detriment or our benefit. Our countries came to exist for the benefit of people within no more than people without.

If Western countries retain any role, it is to work against racism.

We vet prospective visitors and immigrants not for race, as other countries do, but for racism. Not ours, but theirs.

Fundamentally, the West welcomes immigrants because we reject racism: immigration without discrimination. It follows that our compatriots wanting to limit immigration are racist. Overwhelming the last Western loyalists with immigrants might be intended to force us to surrender.

The Open West

Ordinary Europeans who followed our leaders into war in August 1914 soon wanted the war to stop. Our leaders persisted.

Ordinary Europeans did not want war in 1939. If our leaders did not foist war upon us by their blundering and cruelty at Versailles in 1919 or wilfully in 1939, then other leaders did.

Ordinary Europeans did not want immigration. Our leaders imposed it upon us. We imposed it upon Germany, initially.

While hailing our liberalism and democracy, we have become increasingly uninterested in reflecting the wills of white people on matters of race since the Holocaust. We might have majority white populations, but do not deny other races their rights to come and to grow.

Uniquely in the world and through history, the West freely gave up our racially homogenous communities. Races from whom we had kept apart, and who continued keeping each other apart, we admitted into our homelands, suburbs, and streets. Our gates opened wider and wider; our arms were opened to all. We opened our lives to other races, as no other races have.

Nobody invaded. Other races came because our leaders allowed them, even invited them.

When Western countries first loosened our borders after World War II, it seems governments envisaged few people from other races coming to our countries. At least, that is what they told us. We could not imagine many people wanting to become racial minorities, but nor did we imagine so many of them coming that we would become racial minorities.

Had we known then what would come of our countries half a century on, we would not have opened our borders as we did. What has become the most dramatic demographic change of all time was, to the extent our leaders bind us, voluntary.

Indigenous Peoples

The most natural feeling on earth is for people to own the lands of their birth, even if we of the West no longer do, while identifying with their ancestral lands, which we no longer do either. For indigenous peoples, those lands are one in the same. For everyone else, they are not.

The only history of European colonisation and settlement we now countenance is of imperialist invasion, but when colonial Europeans first arrived in North America, Australasia, and elsewhere centuries ago, many indigenous peoples did not feel invaded. Without nation states, indigenous tribes dwelt in their valleys and around their watering holes without staking them out. Nomadic tribes did not even do that, even while fighting with other indigenous tribes.

Europeans setting camps nearby did not affect them, especially when they presumed Europeans were passing by. Conflicts arose when they both wanted the same food and water, much as they did between indigenous tribes.

Having lost faith in our race and Western Civilisation but finding faith in all other races and what we presume to have been their civilisations, we have come to revere indigenous peoples for their lifestyles before we came, without knowing what those lifestyles were. Many of them did very little beyond eating, fighting, and procreating, but they are the people we now believe could have remained wonderful, their societies glorious, if only we had not come. We see much merit in cultures being old, unless those cultures are ours.

Indigenous peoples of Central and South America, especially the Aztecs, Incans, and Mayans with their territorial states and empires, have left legacies of their civilisations. They knew invasion and conquest by Spaniards and Portuguese because they had long invaded and conquered each other.

Normally, an indigenous tribe or race is simply the first tribe or race to have arrived, many millennia ago. The land is no less their ancestral land because of it.

In Australia, there has long been talk and some very small

evidence of a short-statured Negrito race preceding the Aborigines, erased by the Aborigines. For diminishing the Aborigines' stature as Australia's First Peoples, political rejection of the theory has prevented any widespread objective examination of it.

In Europe, hostility to white people means political considerations take the opposite tack. We welcome talk of any race preceding us in Europe, thinking that diminishes our claims to the countries and continent we no longer make anyway.

Land and Identity

Unlike those of us who remained in Europe, we whose forebears sailed from Europe to build our mother empires do not reject nationalism and self-determination altogether. Instead, with no sense of the one-world openness that begs us to welcome other races' immigration into the West, we insist upon nationalism and self-determination, but not for us. We declare what had been our lands still to be countries with borders, but not our countries.

In our devotion to other races and our hostility to our own, colonial Europeans now declare our countries to be and have been all along the countries of the indigenous people, which we invaded. Indigenous people agree.

The time since immigrants came to our countries is supposed to be reason for us to feel comfortable about them being around us, but the much longer time since European colonisation of other lands is not reason for indigenous people to feel comfortable about us having come, or indeed for white people to feel comfortable about being there. It is another of the contradictory standards applied to the detriment always of white people.

While we presume modern-day immigrants all become Americans, Canadians, Australians, and New Zealanders, we presume European colonists never became Americans, Canadians, Australians, or New Zealanders. We no longer feel the lands to which we were born, which our forebears built for them and for us, are ours.

Colonial Europeans pay great heed to the races we call indigenous and their need to link with their land, according them collective ownership to defined areas now unimaginable for us. Europeans in our new homes allow them something of their countries, with rights to discriminate against others, including us. We allow them borders to exclude other races, including us, and even exclude other tribes of their race.

Their land is their identity, they tell us. It is who they are.

We could say the same for white people, but no longer do. The desire for a homeland is human nature we respect for indigenous peoples, but we reject for the West.

Without land, we lack identity, definition: something to ground us. Without a country, what have we? We have nothing.

Selective Borders

If colonial Europeans owe such copious regret to the indigenous peoples whose lands we entered, then the immigrants we graciously allowed to come owe us gratitude. There is no reason for colonial Europeans to leave the New World, those countries we built, unless more recent immigrants leave too.

As it turns out, those immigrants do not owe us gratitude. Instead, we owe them apologies for not admitting them sooner. Nobody cares that their countries are still not admitting immigrants.

Borders we refuse to recognise to keep other races immigrating to the West, nevertheless stand stark in the sky when we remember our colonial period. Ignoring borders here in the present, we imagine borders that were not there in the past.

We denounce our forebears for entering other peoples' homelands uninvited, not complying with laws where there were no laws with which to comply, breaching borders where there were no borders to breach. We damn our forebears still further for keeping other immigrants in check.

Indigenous peoples did not give up their homelands as we now give up ours, as they often remind us and as we often recall. We respect them fighting our colonial forebears in defence of their land, presuming they are right to deny us a welcome we would be wrong to deny other races. Their rights to prevent us coming were not rights we had to prevent other races coming.

If we honoured our ancestors as we honour other races' ancestors, we would respect not just our indigenous hosts. We would respect our forebears who created our countries inviting to others, many dying to defend them.

Instead, we are a string of ideologies by which we advance other races at the expense of our own. So consumed are we with what we can do for other races, we insist immigrants and their successive generations feel greater rights to be in Western countries than we allow ourselves to feel in colonial European countries. We are immersed in self-sacrifice: deferring to everyone else, demanding nothing in return.

Immigration outside the West

The post-racial, post-religious, post-national future we demand is for white people only. Other races agree.

Immigrants advocating immigration, multiculturalism, and diversity for the West are not advocating it for the countries they or their forebears left: their ancestral homelands. They are not letting their landscapes become multiracial as they make ours.

Races other than ours took up our sense of a West without borders, but not our desire for a world without borders. They understand the need for boundaries around their countries; the boundaries nobody respects are Western. Sometimes, they see the benefits of boundaries within countries too.

The most striking verification for the failings of immigration comes not from the countries that embraced it, as from the countries that have not. We might have imagined them following our Western lead, giving up their people and countries into a big global pot. Seventy years after the West began our multiracial dream, other countries are still not buying into it. Our great gesture has not moved them to take the course we have taken.

It has not happened, not even once. While we tirelessly insist that diversity is our greatest strength and that immigrants enrich us, not a single country outside the West wants the same. Not a single country outside the West has opened its borders as we have.

We think refusing other races immigration into our countries would make them our victims, but we do not imagine ourselves victims of other races denying us immigration to their countries. The only nations we reject are our own.

We think that our past emigration requires us to accept immigration. Other races do not think the same of their emigration, past or present.

Races all over the world conquered each other, often colonising each other, without either the conquerors or the conquered thinking that conquest invited the conquered into the lands of their conquerors. That is, except us, but only when we were the conquerors.

Even without empires to aid them, most, perhaps all, races moved around the globe, to the extent they could. In recent years, that has been primarily to the West. Longer ago, the more entrepreneurial races enjoyed the opportunities European empires afforded to pursue wealth for themselves. Without thought of spreading civilisation, Chinese, Indians, and others became prospectors, shopkeepers, and traders across most continents and oceans, even a little in Europe. For the most part, they stayed.

The few countries outside the West incurring immigration, as we understand it, restrict it to their race or religion. Many do not even allow people of their race to immigrate back home.

Modern Japan

When we of the West laud our new-found multiculturalism but say nothing of race, we reduce people to their most visible behaviour: language, cuisine, style of dance. Other races do not.

East Asians, in particular, value racial homogeneity and conformity, believing it aids them economically, socially, and culturally. They are right. Their countries remain pure and secure.

Japan responded to its low birth rate by opening its doors to immigrants, but only those racially Japanese, wholly or substantially: descendants of Japanese émigrés who set out to settle in Japan's empire or in Europe's empires. In a very small way, for they make up a very small percentage of the Japanese population, their return gives Japan a little multiculturalism without multiracialism. By law, race, not place of birth, underpins Japanese citizenship.

Culture can change over generations. Race does not.

Japan allows foreigners to work or study in Japan and foreigners there long enough can obtain permanent residency, but the criteria to obtain citizenship are high. Few bother applying. Most numerous among the immigrant citizens are Japanese-born

Koreans, whose forebears arrived when Japan ruled Korea before 1945, often involuntarily to work.

Japan is not otherwise open to immigrants. It is only partly open to tourists and business travel.

Public venues in Japan declare themselves open only to Japanese. Their stated reason is that other races would not want to enter those venues, although they do not ask us whether we want to enter.

Japan remains Japanese. Japan exists.

Speaking at the Kyushu National Museum in Dazaifu in 2005, future prime minister Tarō Asō said Japan was "one nation, one civilization, one language, one culture, and one race." Japanese do not defer to their indigenous Ainu any more than to immigrants.

If we want to imagine what Western countries would have been like without interracial immigration, we could consider Japan, although our countries would have had more open spaces than has Japan. We too could have shared our prosperity with our people, restoring and maintaining our cities and towns. We too would have weathered natural disasters without widespread looting, as did Japan with the Tōhoku earthquake and tsunami in 2011. Comparing Japan with the West's later decline, it is easy to forget that Japan lost World War II.

Societies

We have no thought of societies. Other races do.

We value individuals, particularly individuals from outside our races. Other races value their communities, rather than individuals from outside their races. They are not mere individuals but peoples, comfortable with their countries, cultures, and races: their racism and nationalism.

More sensible than we are, other races think of themselves. Much more moral than we are, they honour their ancestors. They care for their compatriots and descendants.

They favour their people wanting to prosper, ahead of others wanting prosperity. They retain what they have by discriminating against others. Their people protect them.

Their races enjoy governments defending them. Outside the West, governments and even brutal dictatorships at least claim to defend and advance their national and other racial interests. They do not confuse economic with political liberty, so can grant one but not the other. Those that grant freedoms and fraternity do so for their citizens foremost, not anyone else. They stand with their dominant races against minority races and with both against outsiders. Their nationalism matters more than whatever political systems they employ.

Community

The shortages and rationing brought upon us by World War II continued long after the fighting finished. In spite of suffering two world wars through the preceding half century, by the 1950s or if not then the 1960s, we in the free West again enjoyed good lives. American neighbourhoods were alive with children, mothers' tennis matches, neighbourhood barbecues, community television nights, and overflowing churches.

Australians left our rear doors open for neighbours to visit, talking over tea at kitchen tables. We knew our neighbours and strangers were kind, ready to help. We did not study as hard as Jews and some Asians now study, but we were at least as clever without it.

The gentlest and most civilised nationalism was our quintessentially Western sense of community: a warm expression of a collective sense, with loyalties and sympathies. We helped each other when one of us fell.

When a community was large enough or when several communities coalesced with our civilised nationalism, we called it society. When a society was large enough or when several societies coalesced, we had a country.

Without people to tell them about it, people who were not there do not know what community was only a generation or two ago. The real measures of community were not our relationships with people we knew, but our relationships with people we did not. We knew our communities by people the first time we saw them. The eyes of passers-by met and we smiled. People paused to speak to strangers in the street, or on a bus, tram, or train. We conversed.

Older people know what we used to be like, but few facts are more certain to cause outrage than those pointing out we were happier before other races came. We came to think good lives were a right, but the more we embraced other races, the less we embraced each other.

Our open arms to the world have not brought us connectedness with other races, while we have lost connectedness with each other. We global citizens turn more to the world but less to our neighbours, holed up in their homes beside ours. We do not bother caring for neighbours or what neighbours think of us, when we know we will not be neighbours for long. Strangers stay strangers who do not answer the door.

Residential neighbours have become like everyone else in the individualist West, passing through other people's lives. We no longer look over our fences to wish our neighbours good day, but to check they are not breaching by-laws.

No longer have many of us the comfort of community. All we have are our friends, perhaps family, and other small relationships between small individuals: the people we know, and only some of them.

People fortunate enough to retain strong and supportive communities are happy. Without racism or nationalism, the most that our tribalism can be is localism: our village, town, or neighbourhood. Localism can be very comforting and very supportive, but it is also very small.

Community was not universal. It was another Western trait we lost. No community can admit all comers and remain a community.

Loneliness in Diversity

When immigrants were few, we befriended each other. Most instances of friendships between races around the world arise in environments where the dominant race is Western.

Divisions between races were supposed to fade away over time, but the more people of other races came, the fewer friends we have among them. Understandably, they would rather spend time with their race. They now have more chances to do so.

In spite of our best efforts, and we have tried very hard, racial diversity leads inextricably to a withdrawal from collective life, driving people apart. It reduces trust both between races and within races.

Community groups have come to have less trouble raising funds than they have finding volunteers to carry out chores. White people are more likely to volunteer than people from other races, but we do so more in white areas. Elsewhere, we tire of assisting people who never reciprocate.

Other races are less altruistic than we are, although we refuse to be so racist as to notice. Furthermore, they typically confine their lesser altruism to their friends, families, race, or religion, as we reduce to confine our altruism to ours.

Community requires racial homogeneity. In spite of our repeated claims otherwise, there is no unity in diversity.

For people of different races and religions to find unity, they need a common purpose. They might find a common purpose carrying out particular tasks at hand, but even then only sometimes. Winning a football game or even a team championship might be such a purpose, but even then only sometimes.

Unity requires commonality about something. Community, society, and nationalism require commonality about something.

Diversity leaves people disparate and divided. Whether or not racial and cultural diversity are theoretically compatible with being a civilisation, society, or community, they have proven in practice to be incompatible.

If we had only allowed our race and related races to immigrate, we would still have communities. We would continue to have countries.

To those of us immersed in our tiny little lives, losing community does not matter. With no need to rely upon our neighbours keeping watch on our behalf from loss, we buy burglar alarm systems. We want our neighbours to leave us alone. If we do not live in suburban solitude, we live in rural seclusion. That is individualism.

Solitude makes us comfortable only when we are separated from our tribal human nature. Some people never become comfortably alone. Perhaps no one does. Individuals cannot be anything but alone.

What were our countries have become lonely places. Not content with aloneness, our humanity leaves us lonely. We grab the friends we can to hold for as long as we can. If one or more among our friends are from another race, then we think we are better for the racial diversity around us, but we never wonder what friends we might have had in a homogeneous home.

A city does not cease being lonely for the friends we make. The spaces between strangers make it lonely.

The only companionship we feel is from our proximity to the activity of strangers. People around us with whom we have no commonality, except perhaps solitude, only make us more alone. People we do not know leave us feeling far apart.

When we lost our nations, we lost everything we valued. We lost our societies, communities, and homes.

There is no global village. Western countries are not villages of the world. They are not villages at all. What remains without nationalism is not some unified humanity, but individualism.

Where everyone is individualistic, there are no insiders. Everyone is an outsider, but only some of us realise it.

In a generation or two, we of the homeless West have become the most private people on earth, living in solitary confinement. Amidst all that we have – our ideals and riches – we are alone, condemned by our politics of globalism: individualism. Ours is the Age of Isolation: the smallness of one.

Ethnic Communities

When we began welcoming immigrants from other races en masse, some of us warned that interracial immigrants would not integrate into Western societies. Our governments and the rest of us fobbed off those warnings.

In spite of all the evidence otherwise, including countries outside the West, we are supposed to think other races like diversity as much as we do. They do not. Money and other incentives lead people to emigrate to where they are racial minorities. There, they gather by race.

When white people cluster by race, we call it racism. When other races cluster by race, we call it ethnic based.

We respect other races' sense of togetherness we no longer feel for our own. Not only do we respect their racial togetherness, we fund it.

Applauding Westerners saying race did not exist suited immigrant races when it facilitated interracial immigration to the West. As immigrant numbers grew, they increasingly asserted themselves. Demands for inclusion of others by us in what were our countries, clubs, and everything else gave way to others excluding us in those same countries, clubs, and everything else.

For white people, multiculturalism is symptomatic of our separation from our forebears and rest of our race: our individualism and immorality. For people of other races, multiculturalism for the West expresses their connections with their forebears and race: their racism and morality.

When immigrants do not integrate with us or each other, we do not blame the immigrants. We blame white people. We reject any notion that races failing to assimilate with us or each other can be anything but a failure of government policy or a result of racism: not theirs, but ours.

White people refuse to recognise that people of other races prefer to congregate with their own. It defies our presumption that the only problems of multiculturalism are white people.

There is no melting pot; people do not want it. It is not white people's fault. It is not anybody's fault. It is human nature, but we of the West have become hostile to human nature.

White people have become too individualistic to integrate with each other, but we are devoted to multiculturalism so keep trying to integrate with other races, even while they have no interest in integrating with us. They come to our countries and schools, but not to our school and other social events. They have their own school and other social events, which we facilitate trying to make them feel welcome.

In our quest for inclusion, we invite them to our social events too. Few, if any, of them come. That is their right, although we make excuses for why they do not come rather than acknowledge even to ourselves that they do not want to come. We see people of other races in the shops or student information nights at school and think they are fulfilling our fantasy of a multiracial community.

We presume their children will engage with our children, before becoming like us as adults. Their children do not. Their children remain like them, even if they think their children do not remain enough like them, as parents often do of their children.

There is a plethora of little indigenous and immigrant communities of men and women, boys and girls: pockets of parallel, sweet racial eddies, spinning around in small spaces. They gather among their kind.

Multiracial reality is racial ghettoes, whether poor or affluent. If people cannot find unity, they are lonely. They lose themselves in alienation.

Other races have never been more emboldened. Their unity is often palpable, along with the power it brings them. They are never alone.

The only people without communities are white. We are individuals.

Our individualism leaves us powerless. White people have no unity; that would be racism.

It makes us all the more peculiar that we do not congregate by race. People of other races enjoy their right of free association, to be among their race and to feel better about it. Whether it is merely a matter of taste, as human nature can be, or more, we only damn white people feeling the same, who would if we could.

Multiracial Communities

White people have long become minorities in many places once ours. We still are not minority groups.

The individualism we require of ourselves, we do not require from other races. We bandy about talk of community to describe other races as we would never talk of Britons or Europeans comprising communities, except in Britain or Europe. That is Britain or Europe defined not by race or a collection of races, but by place of residence.

We define Britain and Europe with all the races in residence. Anything else would be racist.

The meaning of our multiracial communities the way we have come to speak of them, or even what we want community to mean, is not clear. In our geography, it is our presumption that we all get along.

Enthusing endlessly for multiculturalism, we consider our multicultural cities cohesive, inclusive, and vibrant, without imagining what they would have been had they remained homogeneously ours. If we think communities or countries can be multiracial, then it is because we have become lax in our interpretation of what communities and countries can be. By any substantive meaning of either, connecting people together, there are no multiracial communities or countries.

Integration is a white people's vision. Multiracial communities are a Western dream.

Ours are the communities more fictitious than real, embracing people of all races alike. We do not imagine them otherwise.

Races not being in open warfare are enough for us to smile with our supposed multiracial community. Even in open warfare, we blame ourselves for not doing more to bring everyone together.

Racial harmony means races not getting in each other's way, leaving each other alone, while solitary white folk frequent their restaurants. Friction between races we can normally ignore.

When talk turns to the problems of racial diversity, immigration advocates plead for cultural understanding. In practice, cultural understanding means refusing to understand. It is a refusal to think about culture, or to feel anything but good about other cultures. If we judge, we judge immigrants by their food instead of anything else.

When called upon to explain why we like immigration, we say it is for the food, but we do not need immigration for food. Our chefs can prepare the cuisines of other cultures and races, if we want them. Chefs outside the West prepare and serve Western and other foods foreign to them, without immigration. At best, multiculturalism is social dislocation, which no number of sushi bars overcomes.

Homogeneity

Racial diversity is for white areas. Other races do not want it for their areas. Our embracing of other races does not mean they do. They prefer the presence of their people.

Each race gathers in its streets or suburbs, its places to belong, but us. Streets and suburbs progress through multiculturalism to become racially one race or another, but not ours.

Places no longer ours become other people's places. Other races assert their homogeneity, as best as they can, as we refuse to defend ours. There is no racial integration but a natural segregation into racial enclaves we are not so racist as to notice, unless we like it.

While discussing the problems of multiculturalism would be

racist, we have no qualms about calling the remnants of white racial homogeneity a problem. Consumed as we are with contempt for our race and thus our dogmatic desire for diversity, suburbs and towns remaining homogenously white have become a fault.

Suburbs and towns becoming homogeneous with other races are wonderful. We think the streets of our cities they occupy are vibrant for no other reason than the occupants no longer being us.

While we speak disparagingly of white streets, suburbs, and cities and the racism they imply, we rarely speak of streets, suburbs, and cities now being of an immigrant race or the racism that implies, except to presume that white racism confines other races there. We call their streets, suburbs, and cities multicultural, which blinds us to how racially homogenous they have again become, but with a race no longer ours.

All multiculturalism and racial diversity really mean are a lack of white people. The fewer the white people where once only white people were, the more multicultural we call a place. We call places that have become wholly of another race diverse, rather than be so racist as to notice their new homogeneity.

The Costs of Diversity

Western countries are no longer lands to belong. Ours have become lands to do business: no longer homes but workplaces.

Throughout the West, we are mindlessly convinced that immigration benefits us economically. It is not true.

Much of our failure to recognise the costs of immigration comes from our refusal to distinguish between races, and between past and present. Our forebears built countries and even empires, with homes, buildings, and infrastructure. Our colonial forebears conquered frontiers.

Present-day immigrants are the easy immigrants, coming to countries already in place, with jobs, charities, and government payments. They occupy homes, hospitals, and schools we have already built. They might help us build more, especially tall apartment buildings, if we pay them to do so, but not for us to live in and use. Nor are they for those immigrants to live in and use, but for other immigrants to live in and use. They are not building all the premises that all the immigrants occupy.

We are no longer building our nations. Why would they?

Immigration stimulates economic activity, which we want it to do, but it lowers per capita productivity growth, a key to sustainable economic growth. It retards per capita wealth. Economic growth due to immigration comes with our per capita economic decline.

We provide healthcare when immigrants fall sick. We provide healthcare when they do not.

Educating immigrant children from under-developed countries requires us to redress their years without adequate education. It thus costs more than educating children coming from developed countries.

Without spending that money and often even with spending that money, educational standards fall. Spending that money, costs rise.

Our only thoughts are economic, but immigration costs us no less in social terms than economic ones. Along with charities, all levels of government expend extra time and money trying to engage people of particular races and religions with programmes and other measures, supporting their clubs and other associations, hoping to keep them from crime, terror, and other wrongdoing.

It is not working. We never expended vast sums of money and effort trying to keep immigrants from within our race from becoming criminals and terrorists, as we have spent upon immigrants from other races.

Our refusal to link race or culture to crime means we do not consider increased policing, security, surveillance, and intelligence costs in the economics of immigration. Some races and cultures increase those costs more than others.

Those costs of immigration include costs that economic analyses do not consider. Immigration accelerates the rate of food importation. It accelerates the increase in urban crowding and traffic congestion. It lowers food security.

Some costs of immigration apply to immigration whatever the race of immigrants. Immigration increases prices to buy or use public assets. It increases prices for products for sale.

Other costs relate specifically to immigrants of other races. Those costs are only exacerbated for immigrants not speaking the host country's language, with additional costs of communication and implementing change.

At the expense of our races if necessary, the West strives to reduce emissions of carbon into the earth's atmosphere. Admitting immigrants from under-developed countries into developed countries increases global carbon emissions in total and per capita.

Businesses beg for more immigration for the sake of their profits, but palm the costs of immigration onto willing governments and customers. We individuals care only about the costs of immigration to us personally. We disregard the costs of immigration to our countries, because we do not think of our countries being ours. The immorality of individualism frees us from caring about the costs of anything to our compatriots.

Immigration and Inequality

Traditionally, socialists and the rest of the political Left opposed immigration for the harm it did working class people. Late in the twentieth century, the Left lost interest in working class people.

The Left stopped believing the poor were poor for being economically exploited by the rich. It bought into the post-Holocaust narrative that other races were poor for being racially exploited by white people, however rich some people of other races were and however poor some white people were.

Whenever we are inclusive of other races, we end up excluding our own. The Left abandoned class struggle to become another forum for racial struggle, against white people. It abandoned white working class people.

The only cohesive theme in the political Left around the West became its hostility to white people. Thus the political Left came to welcome immigration.

The political Right, in spite of its hints and winks to white people come election time, remains merely indifferent to white people. No longer so fearful of communism, the political Right's only remaining interest is economics.

If this Age of Ideology reduces human existence to just politics and economics, then for the political Left it is politics. For the political Right, it is economics.

In national terms, immigration is economically destructive, unsustainable, and immoral, but immigration being against our national interests does not mean it is against everyone's immediate sectional interests. Without nationalism, sectional interests come to the fore.

In our determination to defend immigration, we believe reasons to blame white people for increased home and land prices, but simple economics commands that increases in demand can only pressure prices upward. Property owners enjoy rental accommodation crises, while tenants struggle to find places to live and pay more rent when they do.

Building more homes makes property developers richer. If immigrants are not occupying them, then local people are paying more for the increasing excess of demand to supply. By increasing rental costs, immigration transfers wealth from tenants to landlords.

That is the case for everything, not just housing. Immigration exacerbates an already uneven distribution of incomes, further enriching our rich and impoverishing our poor.

Not merely the uneducated lose from immigration. Educated people lose too.

Immigration and Employment

The political Right first opened Western borders, through the second half of the twentieth century. Big business wanted cheap labour. Rich people wanted cheap servants.

Increasing supply depresses prices, most obviously with labour. The price of labour is wages and salaries. By depressing wages and salary growth, immigration transfers wealth from employees to employers.

We dismiss the bad deeds of immigrants because white people do bad deeds too, but enthuse for the work any immigrants do as if white people do not work. The economic case for immigration reduces the West to economies enjoyed by the rich paying low wages, assumes work done by immigrants would be left undone without them, and ignores poor white people condemned to unemployment, low wages, or welfare. It dismisses the economic and other detriment due to immigration as mere accusations.

Immigrants curtail the income expectations of people already employed, compelling local people to match them or be unemployed. Employees thus accept lower salaries and wages, increased working hours, or other diminished working conditions.

The people losing most from immigration are not just white people. Children of immigrants already arrived grow up with expectations like ours. If we think far enough ahead to worry about that, we know that more immigrants with lesser expectations will be ready to come.

Immigrants do not need to work to assist employers. Pools of unemployed pressure the employed.

We presume economic growth can be infinite but, for the moment, we are confined by finite customers and jobs. Competing for jobs, any immigrant getting a job is at the expense of a compatriot.

The skills shortages by which the West supposedly needs immigration are of our making. Employers and governments do not expend time to train our unemployed. We train foreigners, either in their homelands through foreign aid programmes or in ours. They can then work either in their homelands or in ours.

We talk of labour shortages to justify immigration benefiting labour markets, but there are no labour shortages and there will always be labour shortages. We import a thousand plumbers because we need plumbers. Servicing those plumbers and their families means we need more builders, electricians, teachers, doctors, and so forth. We import the people we need to service those people, and so need more plumbers again.

Immigration feeds demand for more immigration. It will never be mollified.

The labour shortages for which we bring in immigrants indulge people's luxuries: pointless home renovations, adornments to their restaurant dishes they don't eat, coffee they could easily prepare at home. Immigrants and local people fill unnecessary roles in government and big business bureaucracies or carry out unnecessary projects and schemes.

Immigration caters to rich people's greed and decadence and to our need for something in which to believe. It caters to other immigrants in an endless compounding of demand. It feeds the lies of economic growth overall without economic growth per capita.

If immigrant businesses employ all the immigrants, then what is the point of a country and economy? In any event, they do not. They employ only a proportion of immigrants, typically from their race as we of the West refuse to favour ours.

Far from preferring our people, more often than not we prefer unqualified or inexperienced immigrants because they are cheaper. Presuming races are the same as we do in the West, we are unable to imagine people of other races being less skilled, punctual, or diligent than people of our race. The only differences between commodity candidates for a job pertain to price: the fees and wages we pay. Immigrants cost less.

Proponents of immigration claim Western countries need immigrants because local people are not willing to perform particular jobs, but those proponents are not taking those jobs themselves. They employ others, paying tiny wages only immigrants accept. If they were willing to pay wages a little closer to the salaries they expect to receive, they would find local people (especially young people) willing to work.

We should do what our forebears did and the rest of the world does: work with who we have. We could pay people more money to fill unpleasant jobs. We could train people. We could employ older people instead of leaving them unemployed or under-employed. We might also untuck our hotel bedclothes before getting into bed at night instead of paying those hotels to employ maids to untuck them while we sit long in restaurants eating too much dessert.

Quite how immigrants feel to hear relatively rich white people welcoming them to be their servants and serfs does not perturb those relatively rich white people. When those immigrants and their children are sufficiently numerous, the time will come that it does perturb white people. They will do more than merely perturb us.

Immigration and Welfare

Western borders are open to anyone willing to work or to spend. Either will do.

The Western welfare state is fundamentally incompatible with unilateral immigration. Welfare states can only allow immigration bilaterally between countries with similar welfare regimes, or they invite people to immigrate to take advantage of welfare. Welfare payments become a beacon to people to come to a country not to work and a beacon to people willing to work.

Welfare payments might be at odds with classic free market

economics, but military pensions have long rewarded those who served our countries in war. When World War II engaged whole populations in our national defences, whole populations earned rewards. The free West's welfare states were also a useful defence to the threats and promises of communism through the twentieth century.

Parenting payments and aged pensions were not welfare. They were averaging. They recompensed taxpayers for the times in our lives we needed more government aid than we could provide government revenue.

Parenting payments were effectively loans to aid children who would later work and pay taxes in repayment. Aged pensions were a return to people who had worked and paid taxes through their adult lives.

Paying welfare to our people expressed traditional nationalism. It depended upon the recipients feeling reciprocal nationalism: they would work and pay taxes if and when they could. They would again defend our countries if required.

Paying welfare to immigrants has no rationale. It gives money to people who have not developed or defended national wealth and have no reason to do so. There is no reason to pay for the raising of children who will never pay taxes. There is no reason to pay pensions to people who have not previously paid taxes.

Without nationalism or other tribalism joining benefactors and beneficiaries, beneficiaries feel no sense of mutual obligation with benefactors. Able-bodied recipients can choose not to work, or to work secretly while taking welfare payments as if they did not work. Western disability pensions do not keep immigrants from holidaying anywhere on earth.

There is no sense of mutual obligation between races, but not only do immigrants feel no reciprocal obligation towards us. Without nationalism, neither do we individuals feel reciprocal obligations to each other, anymore.

Providing welfare payments to people without the reciprocal nationalism inspiring them to work and pay taxes if and when they can work is unfair upon taxpayers funding that welfare. Paying pensions to people who have not previously paid taxes to that country is similarly unfair. Without nationalism giving us reason to care for our taxpaying compatriots, none of that discourages us from inviting immigration with welfare.

Immigration and Taxation

Refusing to distinguish between races and cultures, we welcome immigrants presuming they will work and pay taxes as we do. Many of them do not work. Many of those who do work do not pay the taxes we pay.

Immigrants might come to the West to be richer (or for their children to be richer) through jobs, government welfare payments, education, or medical and other resources. They might come for beaches, weather, or other aspects of our lifestyles. They do not come to maintain our lifestyles for us or our children.

Immigration might initially provide tax revenue from immigrants of a particular age and vocation, but even those immigrants pay less money in taxes over time than they consume in government welfare and services. If we want immigration to provide tax revenue, then that includes immigrants paying taxes to support previous immigrants.

Much like the argument around labour shortages, immigration feeds demand for more immigration that will never be mollified. Immigration is an insatiable beast.

Governments expending their proceeds of taxation upon immigrants mean local people receive less government benefits in return, unless those governments increase the tax burden upon local people. Governments pass their costs along to unwilling ratepayers and taxpayers, who cannot see what is behind their rates and taxes. If taxpayers do not immediately bear the costs imposed by immigration, then governments compound their levels of debt.

Without nationalism, our only interests in taxation are in the taxes we individuals pay. If we do not pay taxes, or do not think about the taxes we do pay, we do not care about the costs upon government imposed by immigration.

We do not care about the taxes our compatriots pay. We might even like them paying more.

There being no sense of reciprocal obligation between races, simply because we have worked and paid taxes to help other races, or watched while our compatriots worked and paid taxes, is no reason those immigrants who do work should pay taxes to keep us, now or when we age. Rather than providing for us, they have their families and races to keep.

We keep them too. Government expenditures providing for

elderly white people who spent decades paying taxes are already becoming increasingly redirected towards aiding other races. We call it equality.

Equality was never more inequitable. Without white people, the Western cradle will not always be.

Immigration and Individualism

Immigration depends upon powerful white people's complete disinterest in the opinions, rights, and well-being of other white people. The opinions, rights, and well-being about which we care are our own.

Individualism led the West to embrace racial diversity. Conversely, diversity exacerbates our individualism.

Racial diversity broke down much of our collective trade union culture, to the great glee of employers and further disadvantage of workers. It broke down all our co-operative culture.

Any benefits of immigration, if they exist, are tiny, and not for local people. They are for immigrants. That is why immigrants come.

Immigration is a boon, but not for us. Our doctrine of the individual credits immigrants with coming to improve their individual lives, although they come also to benefit their families' lives and their races to whom they remit benefits home, as we individuals of the West cannot comprehend. They would not come otherwise.

If immigration proves not to be good for the immigrants, they return home. Some do, disappointed with their experiences. They have the right to decide. We do not.

Other immigrants keep telling us how awful life is for them at the hands of our alleged racism, but they do not return home to escape it. We strive to ease their supposed distress, while more immigrants keep coming.

Life supposedly being hard for immigrants is no reason for us to withdraw our invitation. It is reason for us to try harder to help them.

The onus is upon us to help the newcomers, as it is not upon us to help each other or upon the newcomers to be responsible for themselves. We nod sympathetically when immigrants accuse our countrymen of racism and we march with them when we can, while we condemn our compatriots feeling aggrieved by immigration for being supposedly lazy and selfish.

Only immigrants and we are allowed to be selfish, not our compatriots. The immigrants we welcome compete not with us, but with our compatriots. Our individual self-interests matter more than other individual self-interests. Our compatriots' self-interests do not matter at all.

We say it has all been worthwhile if the immigrants fare better than they would have fared in their countries of origin. If immigration benefits immigrants more than it costs our compatriots then it improves the lot of the human species overall. It does not matter to us that the winners so often are not white and the losers so often are. Worrying about that would be racism. We think it is fair that immigrants benefit at our compatriots' expense.

We do not even mind if our compatriots lose more culturally and economically than the immigrants gain, so the human lot is worse overall. We of the ideological West cherish interracial equality more than we want our race to be rich or our poor to be coping.

Immigration has left poor white people poorer, without a country to care, but so proudly have we abandoned nationalism, we care nothing for our countries that might no longer exist or the people who could have been our compatriots. We do not think of us having compatriots at all.

If we are not in denial about the impact of interracial immigration upon our races and countries, then it is because we do not care. All our compatriots can lose from the whole immigration process provided we think we gain personally, however little our gain happens to be. We do not even need to gain personally, provided we think we do not personally lose.

We do lose: socially, culturally, and economically. Indiscriminate immigration undermines the economic structures that help us carry on business. It is de facto deregulation. Western borders become more pesky regulations.

So much the individuals, those of us who do not revel in our downfall, just observe. We remark and prepare presentations to audiences more interested in the tea or coffee at the break coming soon.

Individualist Imperialism

Without the reservations of their predecessors, Western governments no longer assume few immigrants will come. Governments and other self-centred interests want more immigrants.

Interracial immigration harms the host nation, while free trade provides any benefits that immigration might offer. Countries outside the West understand.

We are not trying to understand. Without nationalism, we of the West see not just our countries but also the world in terms of our acutely individual interests. Other people are no more than means for individuals to exploit. So are countries. So is the world.

The West remains an age of empires, in which national empires gave way to individual, egocentric empires. Ours are the empires of one: ambitious politicians, judges, and bureaucrats welcoming immigrants to the West for the kudos it gives them currying favour in their supranational careers. Each individual's triumph is his or her race's defeat.

Multiracial immigration does not reflect white people's love for immigrants. It reflects white people's scorn for each other.

Immigration involves not just our willingness to give up our countries, but our enthusiasm for doing so. Pursuing multiculturalism through immigration, we are not blind to race. We want other races: a rush of new arrivals. We lose our countries to the colonisers by the collaboration of our compatriots.

Refugees

For centuries, Europe and her colonies granted refuge to fellow Europeans and to Jews evading religious persecution because we kindly chose to grant it, suffering no harm because of it. They were immigrants, temporarily or not, at a time immigration was rare.

Through the 1930s, they became so numerous as to become a new class of people: refugees. Through World War II, we granted refuge to still more races.

The refuge that Australia generously granted tens of thousands of Asian refugees during World War II was only for wartime. After Japan's defeat in 1945 and our liberation of their homelands, we returned them to those homelands.

We accepted thousands of Jewish refugees from Nazi Germany in the 1930s, but did not accept them all. For those refugees we did not accept, the subsequent Jewish Holocaust led to the United Nations Convention Relating to the Status of Refugees in 1951.

The 1951 refugee convention was a Cold War response to communism, which we recognised then to be as cruel to everyone as Nazism had been to Jews. Signatories to the convention envisaged it applying only to Central and Eastern Europeans, as well as Jews, fleeing East European communism.

Refugees did not really need to be fleeing. They needed only to be leaving.

No less ideological and devoid of nationalism and morality than the communists, the individualists of the political Right increasingly admitted into the West anyone leaving communist countries. It was Cold War propaganda, supposedly proving that communism drove people to flee and capitalism beckoned.

A decade later, the ambit of the convention widened to include other European peoples, when America accepted Cubans fleeing the communist revolution in Cuba. Those refugees were largely upper class and white.

Only with the end of the Vietnam War in 1975 did the ambit of the convention widen still further to include refugees from other races. Several Western countries accepted large numbers of Vietnamese presuming they were fleeing communism.

They too were not fleeing. They were simply leaving. It was more Western propaganda, at the expense of the West.

Few Cambodians were able to escape their country when the communist Khmer Rouge took power in 1975. With the overthrow of that regime in 1979, they could escape. Large numbers of Cambodians emigrated to America supposedly as refugees, although communism had ended in their country.

Communism ended in Eastern Europe in 1989 and '91. Vietnam recovered, slowly liberalising its economy. Cuba recovered more slowly. Very few refugees returned home, except on holidays or for business.

No longer were Western countries accepting refugees only for as long as they needed refuge. They had come to stay.

Our Noblesse Oblige

For those of us most able to help others, European noblemen and women traditionally helped their poor who could not help but be poor, before widening that to the poor of all Europe. Title determined traditional nobility.

That was before World War II. Increasingly since then, politics and money determine our postmodern nobility. They determine pretty well everything in our ideological West.

The end of East European communism in 1989 and '91 made the 1951 refugee convention obsolete, if it was not already obsolete. The convention is a Cold War relic, unsuited to an era when people can travel so freely in large numbers and the West has become unwilling to resist other races, for fear of being called racist.

The West could slash and perhaps even end much of the world's human trafficking in an instant by terminating the 1951 refugee convention and ceasing to reward foreigners reaching our lands. We are not willing to do that.

Instead, when the journey from their homelands or places along their way to the West is too dangerous for them, we set off to collect them. If they reach the West, we encourage them to stay. More than simply granting them refugee rights, we beg them to stay.

Instead of poor white people, refugees have become the principal objects of our postmodern affection. They are the homeless West's cause célèbre, expressions of our global noblesse oblige for people rich enough to want someone about whom to care.

Refugees outside the West

Illegally entering Western countries or remaining in them is not normally a crime. Not every illegal act is a crime.

Outside the West, illegally entering or remaining in a country normally is a crime. Illegal immigrants do not cease being criminals by claiming refugee status.

Accepting refugees from other races is not a universal norm. Like the rest of our interracial immigration, it is a uniquely new

Western norm.

Very few countries outside the West have signed the 1951 refugee convention. Those that have, like South Korea accepting North Korean refugees, interpret the convention narrowly. Only the West resettles refugees from other races in any numbers.

India, which has not signed the refugee convention, harbours illegal immigrants from nearby countries it cannot readily keep out. The Citizenship (Amendment) Act, 2019 offered paths to citizenship to religious refugees who had been in India since 2014, but only those from the related races of neighbouring Pakistan and Bangladesh, both of which had been part of British India, and of nearby Afghanistan. Indians reasoned, as the West does not, that Muslims could not have suffered religious persecution in Muslim countries, although people of other religions might have suffered it. India excluded Muslims from being offered citizenship under the law.

Other countries outside the West also harbour refugees they cannot keep out, but give them none of the rights we do. The charity those refugees receive comes primarily from the West, while they await Western hospitality resettling them in the West.

There was a time we advocated Western countries accepting refugees on the basis that we too might need asylum one day, but there is no reason to imagine we would receive asylum from any country that would not accept us to work or spend money, for as long as we did. There is no reciprocity.

Discriminating not by race but also by religion, Malaysia said in 2015 that it would accept three thousand fellow Muslims as migrants over three years from the millions of refugees from the Syrian Civil War. The gesture expressed Malaysia's desire to lead a Muslim world divided between Shia and Sunni, but was still tiny aside the numbers of Syrians that Western countries accepted.

The only other Asian countries accepting refugees from resettlement camps are Japan and South Korea, but the numbers are miniscule. Those countries do not give those refugees citizenship or much else.

Japan explicitly rejects economic refugees, drawn to that country by its wealth. We of the West, on the other hand, remain so certain of the goodness and bona fides of other races that we refuse to believe refugees are drawn to our countries by our wealth.

Unskilled Immigration

While communist countries generally forbade emigration, they did allow some people to leave. The insane, disabled, chronically sick, elderly, and repeatedly criminal were often free to depart, for a West that cared for them as communists did not.

Refugees were the worst of a people. They still are.

Since we became so welcoming of refugees and other immigrants, the Third World has become rife with people seizing any opportunity to enter the West. Criminals might simply need to leave where they are.

Most illegal immigrants reaching the West have passed through several countries along the way, but asylum in the West is a much better offer. Knowledgeable about Western immigration rules if nothing else, because nothing else offers so much reward, the people we call refugees are not looking for refuge. They are looking for money.

That can be money for themselves, which we ought to understand. With senses of family that we have lost in the individualist West, that can also be money for their families that follow them or money they send home.

People with nothing to offer their countries set off for the West. Immigrants want better lives, as most people do, with refugee status the call for people too poor and unskilled to qualify under other categories of immigration to the West. Asylum is an excuse.

In our globalist vision, impoverished immigrants are just another facet of global impoverishment, indistinguishable from the poor left at home. Yet, wildly confident in the merit of immigrants or consumed as ever by our white man's burden, we blame their continuing impoverishment having reached the West upon our failures to provide for them after they arrive. We do not blame their lack of skills and other traits by which they were already impoverished before they arrived. We do not blame ourselves for impoverished white people who never moved.

The West's refugee regimes are immigration mechanisms like any other, pointed towards the same end along different means. Refugees are the lows in immigration, unless lying and fraud constitute skills. In the postmodern West, they do.

Reasons to Lie

Conscience is a Western concept, albeit one in rapid decline with the rest of Western cultures. Other races write and say whatever serves their interests, without minds behind their mouths sensing their words are untrue, even demonstrably so, as a conscience would sense.

From its earliest days, the 1951 refugee convention facilitated liars and cheats. By the twenty-first century, all asylum seekers are reputedly liars.

Instead of reasons for people to be truthful, we create reasons for people to lie. We insist asylum seekers are telling the truth as if questioning them was a flaw, but their applications to immigrate depend on their answers. Without reason to be truthful, people say whatever they think helps them get what they want.

The most treacherous of illegal immigrants command our sympathies by claiming asylum. With asylum come all the rights the trusting West grants them.

We welcome the persecuted and the persecutors. We welcome people who hate us. Anything else would be discriminatory.

We understand individual interests so well, but only when we are the individuals. We trust people of other races, as we have ceased trusting each other.

Thinking people of other races lie would be racist. We think only white people lie.

Confusing justice with trust, we believe whatever other races tell us to claim our compassion. People lie to enter the West, but if we could fly back through time to 1939, we would not turn away Jews fleeing Nazism for being liars.

From Where Refugees Come

Even the best of immigrants are normally not the best of their homelands, especially when life in those homelands is improving. Successful people do not need to leave their countries, although many do. We encourage them to come to the West.

With patriotism unimaginable in the West, those that remain in their countries often do so to aid their countries. Those countries plead for their people able to work to remain or, if they have left, to return. Few return, when we give them so many reasons to remain in the West.

Countries complain most about losing their educated émigrés to the West, preferring that we take their lowliest, laziest slum-dwellers. We take them, too.

There will never be solutions to other countries' problems while we admit into the West the people who could solve those problems. They are most obviously the fittest and healthiest young men who fill refugee flows, uneducated and unskilled they might be.

Granting people refuge from regimes should mean we cease giving those regimes foreign aid, favourable trading terms, and the rest of our unbridled generosity, but we continue doing so. We applaud our relationships with countries, while granting asylum to their citizens. It would have been much like granting refuge to Jews fleeing the Holocaust, while lauding our relationship with the Nazis.

Indeed, we acknowledge the offence to other countries that granting refugee status to their citizens can cause, if they do not realise what a free-for-all the refugee industry is. We grant refugee status nevertheless. We just might not mention it.

If we think circumstances are so dire or oppressive in a country that justice or mercy demands we admit refugees from that country, then it beseeches us to aid and protect the people those refugees left behind. When those refugees are fleeing a tyrannical regime or invading force, then granting refuge should mean we are willing to go to war against that regime or force. We went to war with Germany and Japan through World War II. We maintained a readiness to go to war with the Soviet Union and Cuba through the Cold War.

We are not willing to go to war with the countries from which today's refugees come: to return to empire over those countries. Granting refuge is a weak lazy response, for a West that cares as little for other countries as we care for our own.

An Ideology Called Compassion

The West has become fixated with money. We have also become consumed with a romantic, idealised view of other races. As if admitting a fault in our fixation with money, we cannot imagine other races also being fixated with money.

Other races are fixated with money, although to a much lesser extent than we are. They are not willing to lose their countries for money. They are quite willing for us to lose our countries for them to get money. So are we.

Behind the refugee industry lie the same sectional elite commercial and political interests wanting other immigration. The corporate leaders we condemn in other contexts are the corporate leaders we trust when they want the West to admit refugees. Wealthy white men and women flaunt their supposed virtues by calling for more refugees and immigrants to come, while José tends to their gardens and Mai-Ling cleans their houses.

The immorality of individualism is as central to the West resettling refugees from other races as it is to the rest of our indiscriminate immigration. Every right we give others comes with a cost, but we think we only suffer what we suffer individually. Thinking we lose nothing whoever might come, we care nothing for our ignoble compatriots struggling to deal with their declining lives, provided we hold true to our individual selves.

In the height of our selective compassion, we believe every story of suffering from strangers seeking asylum, but not bother with testimony from our compatriot victims of crimes that refugees commit. White people suffering harm from refugees no longer enter our thinking. We are uninterested in facts that do not accord with our convictions we are compassionate for welcoming refugees.

Safely secure in our tucked-away homes, we sit snug in our sofas, away from the streets we create. Feeling good for ourselves, we are generous with other Western lives.

Generosity to other races does not make us kind people, because our thoughts are not of people. There is no love in welcoming refugees claiming persecution without regard for the impact of them coming on people already here. There might be reason they are persecuted. They might not be persecuted at all.

We were compassionate, before we touted our compassion. Without nationalism, the West lost our grace and compassion.

For all our demands for compassion by others, individualism fosters little compassion in practice. We are no longer compassionate communities, because we are no longer compassionate or communities. Communities are compassionate to their own, but confining compassion to our own would be discriminatory. Refusing loyalties leaves the West without compassion at all.

Instead, we have ideology called compassion: a political expression lying not in our hearts or hands but in our self-aggrandising dogma, most obviously around refugees and other immigrants we demand our compatriots indulge. Our crude compassion is an abstraction we cite to cut each other down, when the other does not share our belief: when he or she does not aggrandise us for our beliefs as we aggrandise ourselves.

Our countries have become refuges for everyone, but us. If refugee advocates felt love, care, or compassion, instead of insisting they did, they would not be refugee advocates. They would be nationalists.

We claim to care so much for other races, but without nationalism or other tribalism, we exploit and oppress our own. We with our nations were kinder people than we citizens of the world have become.

The World's Correctional Services

Limits upon gaining asylum in the homeless West are few. Crimes that refugees have committed before reaching the West are no more reason to refuse them admission to the West than are the crimes they will commit after arrival.

No longer are we only accepting refugees provided our people are not harmed as a result. Vietnamese and Cambodian refugees especially became renowned through the 1970s and '80s for drug trafficking and other crime, although Western authorities denied it at the time. Only later did authorities admit that crime, when those authorities claimed the crime had ceased. Again, Western authorities lied.

We might evict foreign citizens convicted of crimes, but it is selective eviction. We are more likely to deport them to other Western countries than out of the West.

Refusing to discriminate, the impositions and punishments we have abolished for our compatriots we have abolished for everyone else. We do not deport foreign criminals to countries imposing execution, lashings, or other punishments to which we object. We let them stay in our countries. We give them money.

We are not just the world's policemen. We are the world's correctional services.

The logical corollary to the accommodations we grant criminals is inviting the rest of the world to send us its criminals who face punishments we consider too harsh, if that is what they want. We can gaol them in the comfortable West, or impose whatever lesser punishments we consider appropriate.

With morality obsolete in the ideological West, there are increasingly no criminals. They are people with problems: more people to help.

Immigration means importing other country's problems, making them ours. With our white man's burden mentality, we think they already were.

The White Saviour Complex

Without much difficulty, we find reason to designate people wanting to come to the West or to stay refugees. Their telling us they are refugees is often enough, although bureaucrats, courts, and tribunals like a little bit more.

All sorts of claims of danger or disadvantage in a foreign country can found refugee status in the West, even if the same danger or disadvantage exists in the West. Whatever safety or benefit refugees are pursuing is the converse of the danger or disadvantage they are fleeing. They are fleeing any circumstance not as good as their lives could be in the generous West.

The West is a beacon not just for liars and thieves, but for the sexually immoral. From the viewpoint of the immoral West, we perceive persecution in the morality the rest of the world retains.

There are some limits upon being postmodern refugees. They cannot be white.

However much the ideological constructs of the race theorists ought to say otherwise, accusing people of colour of racism is racist, even in the countries they rule. Thus granting white people refuge from that racism would compound that racism.

Seven decades onward, the Holocaust remains at the heart of our accepting asylum seekers, no matter the cost to our countries in doing so. We accept them because we did not accept all the Jews fleeing Nazism before World War II, but there is nothing remotely comparable between Jews fleeing the Holocaust and modern-day asylum seekers. No Jew returned to functioning Auschwitz on holiday, buying souvenirs and taking photographs, as modern-day refugees return to the countries from which we have granted them asylum because they are supposedly persecuted or otherwise in danger there.

For all the failings in the world, no genocides are under way, not outside the West anyway. When there have been genocides, such as in Cambodia under the communist Khmer Rouge, people could not leave the country.

The refugee industry is more marketing of the West's open borders to a gullible Western populace wanting so much to be kind. We are not saving refugees' lives by admitting them to the West, but we remain convinced of refugees' victimhood bona fides because it suits our visions of ourselves.

At the depths of our white man's burden, we are in psychological terms immersed in a massive saviour complex: our White Saviour Complex. We like to feel like we are saving other races, because we are not saving our own.

Human Rights

Rights are a Western invention. Other races do not normally think in such terms.

Initially, rights were grounded in city-states, races, and nations. English rights were for Englishmen and women. Scottish rights were for Scots.

Following World War II, the West insisted upon everyone having rights that Jews did not have through the Holocaust. We deemed rights universal. They became everyone's rights: human rights.

Initially, human rights also remained predicated upon nations and borders. The Universal Declaration of Human Rights, 1948, granted people the right to leave countries without contemplating rights to enter them.

Losing the last of our senses of race and nation over time, we in the West went further than that. No longer reserving rights to our own, we granted more and more rights to the rest of the world, expecting nothing in return. We deemed rights inalienable, as if we do not grant them: the ideology of rights. Entitlement became universal.

Most countries outside the West came to confer on their citizens some individual rights. They might call those rights human rights because they see so many governments granting them, but what they grant, they grant only to their citizens. They might not even grant those rights to all of their citizens, when their citizens include people of other races.

They give foreigners few rights and revoke those rights without appeal when their people's interests require revocation. In effect, they confer only courtesies to foreigners, for as long as they choose.

We plead for human rights everywhere, but only the West believes it. Western countries give more rights to everyone than other countries give anyone. Minorities and majorities share an abundance of rights in the West, more than other countries give their majorities. No other countries confer so many rights on so many people as we do.

In the world of comparative rights, we have fewer rights than other races do. They have our rights in our countries. We do not have their rights in theirs.

Human rights activists, unless they are white, fight for rights for people of their race or, perhaps, religion. They do not fight for people of other races or religions, although people of other races or religions might incidentally benefit. They do so from their residences in the West. They do so elsewhere.

Only we fight for other races' rights. Thus human rights activists wanting more rights for other races will demand fewer rights for us, especially around our freedom of speech to disagree with them: to defend our countries, cultures, and people; to criticise or even question immigration.

Human rights have become for other races' benefit, not ours. There are few surer signs of indifference to Western lives, even hostility towards us, than the phrase "human rights" in a person's profile or job description.

National Rights

The West sees human rights as individual rights, for all individuals. Human rights elsewhere focus upon collective rights, for families, nations, and races: theirs.

Governments outside the West provide collective rights for their countries, not other countries. Racial rights are for their races, not other races. People might not have the individual rights we demand for us all, but neither do people who would harm them.

We have none of the national rights other races enjoy; that would be nationalism. Only Western countries do not make our national interests paramount: our people's lives paramount.

Granting rights to people has consequences, but we are unconcerned about consequences. We just care about rights.

Applying our values to other races is absurd, but no right is so destructive we do not allow it for others. When the rights of white people and rights of people of other races diverge, the rights that come to the fore are not ours; that would reek of old racism. The rights of some people matter more than the rights of others. The rights of other races matter most.

People from other races and nations might harm us but still we refuse to discriminate, not anymore. It is unfair on the innocents and the guilty. The guilty have rights, too.

We surrender freedoms so the people who would harm us have their freedoms. If we have rights not to be victims, our rights do not matter.

In theory, we could care about each other as much as we care about people wanting to harm us. In practice, we do not want any hint of our old ways.

Every right we possess only to the extent our forebears bequeathed it to us and others do not erase it. Making our rights universal and inalienable has not brought us anything we did not already have, or could have had.

If rights are worthwhile, they are in living freely among people at peace. Defending other people's liberties denies us ours.

We do not need more rights we cannot use, but more rights we can. National rights mean offering fewer rights to the rest of the world. If all that seems radical, then it is only radical in the homeless West.

National Obligations

We of the West used to have national rights and personal obligations, as other races still do. We now have personal rights, as other races do, and national obligations, as other races do not.

The only times we talk of Western nations are in the context of our supposed collective duties to others. We take not personal but collective responsibility: rarely countenancing individual obligations, at least upon us, while suffering national obligations aplenty. Granting other races their human rights mean our national obligation is to honour them.

Refugees expect more from the West than just refuge. We agree.

Our national obligations do not end with admitting refugees; granting refuge is not enough. We also provide money, healthcare, education, training, and houses to the standards they demand.

How many poor white people would like the same? We see our national obligations as being to other races, not to our own. If not cruelty, it is our cruel neglect.

While we are uninterested in living with our race, we have great respect for people of other races wanting to live with theirs. We provide them with more money so they can.

Accepting refugees and other immigrants is expensive. The expense never ends.

Immigrants still accuse us of racism for anything we do not provide them. They know their complaints only inspire us to give more.

We do not sense our kindness towards them because we think we have done what we are obliged to do. Their entitlement binds us.

Feeling collective pride for being generous to other races would be racist. Separated as we are from our races and nations, the pride we feel, if we feel any, for what our nations do is personal: for the demands we make upon our nations in which we do not believe. We are not as generous with our meagre houses and apartments as we are with our countries we do not want anyway.

Nationality without Nationalism

Centuries ago, we created nation states. Now, we reduce nation states to paper-thin citizenship, which can change by the stroke of a bureaucratic key.

Nationality means more outside the West, where countries reserve citizenship to their own. They equate nation and race, much as the West does rejecting both. Their countries continue.

In the Western world, nationality no longer equates to race. We freely grant citizenship to people who want it, for as long as they do. There are conditions, but they are conditions people of any race meet.

A practical notion in 1868 when immigrants were Europeans who had arrived by boat and documentation could be scant, the Fourteenth Amendment to the American Constitution conferred rights of citizenship on people born in the country. A century and a half later, children of illegal immigrants exploit that Amendment to argue they are like children of colonial Europeans born lawfully on American soil. They are the anchor babies, trying to secure themselves and their families in America.

Their mothers do not even need to have immigrated, but might want to keep their and their families' options open for possible immigration in the future. Birthing tourism invites foreign women, especially wealthy Chinese women, to fly into America to give birth in American hospitals, before heading back home again.

Without nationalism but with our individualism, ours is single-person citizenship. When a new offer outshines the old, we change Western nationalities, if it suits us to do so.

Single-person citizenship is ours to pick or reject, at a whim. People with no sense of nation still want their countries to bail them out of trouble into which they have dumped themselves, especially in other countries. Those other countries and races are not lauding them as they laud those other countries and races.

The West is not just for sale. It is for sale at fairs. It can come with immigration.

Western citizenships are not a privilege. They are more products for sale.

Needing the permits to live, work, and travel that come with citizenship somewhere, people buy nationality in the West. We advertise it.

Western governments are not the only governments selling citizenship. Ours are the only rich governments selling it. Ours are also the only governments selling it to people we expect to come to our countries, instead of living and tripping around elsewhere.

White people are the only people not to care that their governments sell citizenship. Caring would be racist.

What we do not sell, we give away. American residency can be a game to be won, entirely by chance. We prefer a multitude of races coming through our borders to the days when almost all immigrants were European.

With Western countries trivialising our citizenships, there is little wonder the rest of the world trivialises Western citizenships too. Only race matters.

Passing nationalities mean nothing. People fleeting into countries do not become compatriots because of the forms they file and fees they pay, nor even the taxes we imagine they remunerate. We are not suddenly bonded together and then suddenly not when they fleet out again. If we were, then the bonding was brittle.

Without nationalism, we are not countries. We are landscapes. Western countries become patches and portions of earth, to which anyone can come and remain.

Western citizenships being transient, identities based upon them are equally transient. Central to our new, post-national identities is not being nations at all. Our identities become bits and pieces of land: a street, suburb, or city. We cease being what we were and become something else by changing abode. We are where we live.

Changing identity so readily is superficial and shallow, among people passing through or staying a while. Of all the identities to choose in our post-racial West, none are more facile than geographical identities.

If nationality is a weak identity for being merely a legal descriptor, then geographical identity does not even require a legal right to reside. If accidents of geography are all we have to call ourselves a country, then it is nothing at all.

We have nowhere we belong, just places we reside. We have become itinerant, but we are not nomads by nature. Nations without nationalism do not remain nations for long.

Countries of Immigrants

Colonial Europeans no longer define our countries by our mother countries or Europe. In our rejection of race, it has become fashionable to redefine ours as countries of raceless people called immigrants, however long ago we arrived and however recently other races arrived.

We thus remove our connection to the land, making us less than our indigenous peoples. We also trivialise our forebears who built our countries, sharing their credit with recent arrivals from all manner of countries who might not build anything.

A key distinction remains. Recent arrivals, from outside the West, we do not call invaders as we call our European forebears.

Europe is becoming the same. European countries have begun claiming to be countries of immigrants.

Redefining our countries as countries of immigrants is more than just redefinition without race. It is abandoning all notion of being countries at all. The very fact that someone comes (by whatever means and for whatever reason) makes that person a compatriot. People wanting to come aspire to be our compatriots, so we should let them come too. People wanting to stay are the same.

We are far and away the most welcoming race on earth, although we are not so racist as to believe it. We are the only welcoming race on earth, if welcoming means letting entrants stay for as long as they want to stay, even generations to come.

Other races know we are so nice and welcoming. The West's unilateral niceness entices people to come without thought of complying with our laws.

What other races call invasion, we call immigration, even asylum. Never before have countries or continents invited invasion as the West now does, even funding it.

The End of Country

The 1951 refugee convention acknowledged that people could enter or be in a country legally or illegally. The convention referred to *"illegal entry or presence"* in a country when saying that should not disadvantage refugees.

Illegal entry does not disadvantage refugees in the West. It increasingly does not disadvantage anyone in the West.

The fervent anti-communist presidents Ronald Reagan and the first George Bush granted amnesties to illegal immigrants expecting electoral gratitude for their Republican Party. They did not get it.

Nothing does more to spur illegal immigration than amnesty for illegal immigrants being in the wind. America's amnesties did.

Illegal immigration no longer makes people illegal immigrants, not in the homeless West, because we insist people are never illegal. They might simply commit illegal acts. It is like saying no one is ever a criminal. Some people simply commit crimes, or become involved with the criminal justice system. We accommodate everyone.

People who would be illegal immigrants elsewhere in the world have become undocumented immigrants in the West. We have reduced Western countries to matters of paperwork. Western borders are coming down altogether.

Never are the gall of other races and the weakness of ours more evident than in matters of immigration. People do not need to earn respect from white people as they do from other races. They demand our respect, whatever they have done or will do.

We give it. For us to respect illegal immigrants, they do not need to respect us or our borders. We do not.

We think nothing is fairer and more equitable than giving the same benefits to people who (or whose parents) violated our national borders as we would give our citizens. Corrupting our convictions of universal rights to discriminate in favour of ourselves would be incomprehensible, but we discriminate in favour of others. We give them more than we give our own.

We do not punish illegal immigrants. We help them. We help everyone, but our own.

Liberty for immigrants leaves less liberty for the West. We are increasingly barred from differentiating between legal and illegal immigration. We have no right to exclude and evict anyone, not even those who could harm us.

The trouble with no person being illegal is that no other person can ever be legal. Nobody is excluded. Nobody is included.

A country without borders is not a country; open borders are not borders. Homes for everyone are homes for no one: national nothingness. We do not have countries anymore, but neither does anyone else, not yet.

Democracy and Nationalism

The city-states of Classical Greece broadened the rights and responsibilities of citizenship to, at most, all free adult males of a city. They did not extend citizenship to foreigners, by which each city-state included not just people of other races but Greeks from other city-states.

The democracy sometimes preached in ancient Greece and sometimes practiced in ancient Rome was not universal. It was democracy for Greeks and Romans, and only particular Greeks and Romans. Classical democracy remained for the few for thousands of years, but with nationalism moving the few to exercise their democracy for the common good.

Western countries gradually came to enjoy universal suffrage, but it was universal within races and nations. Democratic power lay with majorities, so that a majority of a majority amounted to control, but a minority of a majority was still a minority. Nevertheless, with nationalism connecting people together, those minorities losing democratic elections respected those majorities winning elections because they too had enjoyed their chances to vote.

With nationalism, those majorities governed for all. Our governments represented our countries. Their primary responsibility was to safeguard their citizenry, or at least purporting to do so.

Much as it does for other good government, democracy depends upon nationalism. Until 1945, we only contemplated democracy within nations. Increasingly since 1945, our homeless West only contemplates democracy without nations.

Without nationalism, we vote without regard for how our vote affects our compatriots. We might never meet people that suffer because of policies we endorse.

Without nationalism, minorities losing elections no longer respect majorities winning them. Majorities no longer govern for all. Only sectional interests matter.

Unsuited to individualism, democracy no longer ensures good government. Democracy is more for the benefit of people elected than for the people electing.

Democracy is a right we enjoy. We do not have the democracy, we have the right: the right to make choices we are supposed to make, from most options alike. Much the same sectional interests dominate whichever political party wins.

Western governments operate beyond democracy's reach. We think we are democratic for being able to vote for whomever we want to vote, from what seems an array of political parties and candidates, but our elections are confined to the choices before us: between parties and candidates who need only position themselves to one side of another, subject to the best marketing they can buy.

Without nationalism to unite us or to ground a conviction in truth and other morality, the practical reality of Western democracy has long left our ancient ideals to become competitive deception. We can only blame the people for some of our governments and fewer still of our laws.

Democracy and Globalism

Most, if not all, countries around the world have ruling classes whose interests and opinions prevail above those of their compatriots. Only in the West do those ruling classes subjugate their races' interests to the interests of other races.

When judges (not normally answerable to democratic elections) ceased expressing national interests but turned to their individual, sectional, or global visions, their independence from other arms of government and the people ceased being a cornerstone of national democracy. Their independence became an impediment to national democracy.

One view holds that judges settle upon what their judicial decisions should be. They then set about justifying them.

Increasingly since World War II, Western courts and governments have imposed their vision of what liberal democracies should be, as if that was what our nation-makers intended, but it is very different (if not diametrically opposed) to anything our nation-makers envisaged. Recasting the meaning of our liberal democracies to be non-discriminatory, without favour to our own, Western courts and governments redefined our democracies to be no longer the wills of our nations, but the will of the world.

They redefined their roles from representing their citizenry to representing the world. Ours became global democracies, representing all peoples' interests: democracy without discrimination. Our Western ideals became universal.

Our visions of a new earth begin with us. We lecture foreign governments what we think they should do but, for the most part, we lead by example.

Governing our bits of geography on the world's behalf, Western governments enact treaties and laws placing the world's interests above those of our countries. Western civil servants administer our countries on the world's behalf.

Thus they assess what other races want of them. Judging by the enthusiasm with which other races take up the chances we give them, Western governments and civil servants are probably right.

Nationalism subordinates foreign relations to national interests. Globalism subordinates national interests to foreign relations.

In foreign affairs, nationalism means expressing the wills of a people to the rest of the world. Globalism means imposing the views of the rest of the world on a people.

Nationalism refuses foreign intervention in a nation's internal affairs. Globalism rejects the concept of a nation's internal affairs, for anything important.

Western governments still take actions to safeguard their citizenry, but not to the disadvantage of anyone else. Anything else would be discriminatory.

With their nationalism and racism and to the extent they feel they need to speak up and act, governments outside the West represent not just their citizenry but their emigres, however many generations ago those emigres left. Their emigres enjoy support from their governments, businesses, and races.

They also enjoy it from ours. Thus, immigrants with citizenship of Western countries might have two governments defending and promoting their interests.

White people cannot count on any. We live knowing we have no one on our side, no one in our corner.

Our governments and compatriots might speak up on behalf of our citizenry in trouble somewhere, but no more than they say on behalf of other citizenry in trouble. By deeming us citizens of everywhere, we become citizens of nowhere.

That is individualism. That is globalism.

Democracy and Immigration

Interpreting much from democratic elections is difficult. People have all sorts of reasons to vote as they do.

Voters might disagree with candidates on issues, but still vote for them. People might agree with candidates on issues, but still not vote for them. We normally do not know voters' second and subsequent preferences. All we can say is that in no referendum or election has a majority of white people clearly and consciously voted for increased interracial immigration.

Many white people have wanted increased interracial immigration. They are often white people living where immigrants do not. Their individualism separates them from white people living near immigrants.

We have our ideals about the way the world and our country should be, but the only ideals worth holding are those we are willing to bring down on ourselves as freely as we are willing to bring them down upon others. No person should vote for more refugees or other immigration unless she is willing to accommodate them in her drawing room.

That powerful people embarked upon their multicultural and single-world visions without the approval of their race only makes them prouder. Governments overrode us.

Every citizen of a Western country could oppose immigration, but our governments would still not respect racism. In the conflict between democracy and diversity, Western governments defer to diversity.

What we used to call democracy, expressing the will of the people, we now condemn for being populism. Populism is democracy for white people.

(Populism is socialism for immigrants. They demand more than we want to give them.)

The political purpose of immigration might simply be votes. In our post-national democracies, immigrants vote for more of their people's immigration. They do not vote for other races' or religions' immigration, unless it suits them.

Ethnic community leaders band together on their concerted behalf for more immigration by all of them. While their community leaders are unlikely to upset other ethnic community leaders and risk their mutual support, some immigrant races recognise that they lose or might lose from other immigrant races coming. What is good for some immigrant races is bad for others.

For all races but ours, self-determination matters more than democracy, when democracy empowers another race. Other races in their countries alter their systems of government to protect their political power.

Only we in our countries alter our systems of government to reduce our political power. We do not just accept racial democracy empowering immigrant races to rule over us. We accelerate it. We call it equality.

White people are not the only races on earth denoting rights by race. We are the only races doing so at our expense.

We are the only races freely giving up our self-determination, accepting of demographic destinies to our detriment. We are handing rule to everyone else.

Voting by Race

In democracy without nationalism, the most important issues are demographic. In multiracial democracies, the first issue is race.

Viewpoints differ between races. Those differences do not cease when we admit other races into our countries. There is no multicultural voice, no global consensus.

Like everything else political, democracy is racial. In multiracial democracies, people vote in accordance with their race and religion. Representative democracy is representation by race.

White people cannot vote for candidates of our race without defending ourselves from charges of racism. People of other races can vote for candidates of their race.

Still believing in the roles of race and religion, other races retain their loyalties. If it is not racial loyalty, it is a sense that candidates from their race understand and represent them better than candidates from another race.

White people have lost our loyalties. We have lost any sense that candidates from our race understand us. Most candidates from our race do not.

That generally means people of other races vote for political candidates from their race, although voters will not vote for candidates they feel will not win the election or whose political party, policies, or other attributes they believe are not the most supportive for them and their race. Candidates from other races can offer more to assist them and their race to win their support. Racial blocs vote according to their racial interests, as they perceive them to be.

We respect other races voting for their own because they are their own, among whatever considerations they take into account. We cater to it, in the candidates our political parties put up.

Passing laws and administering government to the benefit of a person's race is perfectly natural, even if white people no longer do so. We might even prefer laws and administration that disadvantage our race, for the sake of equality.

For all the criticism we mete out upon ourselves, an adage in politics is that racial minorities vote for their race but, all else being equal, they prefer white candidates to those from other races. Other races are not as obliging to each other as we are to all of them. We treat them better than they treat each other. We treat them better than they treat us.

Interracial Socialism

Nations depend upon nationalism. Without nationalism, the result is theft, and worse, by the powerful from the powerless.

Democracy does not help. Without nationalism, democracy empowers the fifty-one percent to elect governments neglecting the forty-nine percent, or worse. It empowers the fifty-one percent to elect governments taking money, property, and everything else from the forty-nine percent.

When the majority is richer than the minority from which it takes, or that it simply neglects, it might call everything free enterprise. With foresight, the majority might try to appease the minority, but cannot when the swelling underclass of servants and beggars, by whatever moniker they are known, eventually becomes too numerous for democracy to deny it.

When the new majority is poorer than the new minority from which it takes, it will call its theft from the new minority something like justice, equality, or socialism. Conversely, that new majority might already be richer than the new minority from which it takes, but still call its theft justice, equality, or socialism.

We have long qualified democracy's majority by demanding respect for racial and other minorities, before Western democracies went further and deferred to minorities. Other racial majorities, in their countries outside the West, do not defer to racial minorities, although they maintain the nationalism by which they defend their own. There is no reason to imagine them deferring to minorities if they ever become majorities in our countries.

Rich and powerful white people, and even white people not so rich and powerful but comfortable, imagine their lives continuing unchanged behind their property walls, while they proudly call for more immigration to the West. They might even promise other races equality with ours, presuming those other races are like us.

However much the West insists otherwise, races are different, cultures are different. Some races work harder than others. Those that work hard, work differently.

Races will never become equally rich by fair competition: by economic, political, and social systems oblivious to race. What ought to be self-evident from observing economic conditions in different countries around the world and in different races within countries is not evident at all, to a West refusing point-blank to consider issues of race and culture.

Sharing cities and countries, races become classes. Most races, other than ours, want equality improving their lot until they get equality. They then want more.

Minority races not getting in our way when they are small do so when they are numerous enough. Substantial enough minorities need not even be majorities to prevail, any more than we deferred to majority opinions when we opened our countries to crowds.

When other races but ours are the majority race or compilation of races, they can democratically vote to strip wealth from the white, Jewish, and any other minority they choose. They can do so from people rich and poor.

However admirable the theory of universal suffrage, in multiracial practice, it becomes manifestly unfair. If we want to imagine such a scenario in our countries when the Europeans who built them no longer dominate, we have Venezuela to consider.

Single World Government

Talk of Continental Europe fell from use when we decided Britain and Ireland were parts of the European continent, following our membership of the European Economic Community from 1973 and especially the European Union from 1992. What were a myriad of countries and cultures throughout Europe, North America, and Australasia have slowly become the near-seamless West.

Worse than that, the West became near-seamless with the rest of the world. Talk of Australasia fell from use for implying something combining Australia with New Zealand without Asia or the Pacific.

Erasing Australia's identity, Australians talk of Australia being in Asia, in spite of them being separate continents. Papua New Guinea is not a continent, is much smaller than Australia, and is closer than Australia to Asia, but Papua New Guineans do not call themselves part of Asia.

Those who would give up their countries and the West might give them up into a dream of a single world civilisation of whatever nature. They might simply give them up.

When the West fantasises about open borders, the logical consequence is a single world government: a very Western thing to want. Many a Western business leader shares the dream of a worldwide superstate for the limitless markets of labour and buyers. Critics of capitalism would let businesspeople have their limitless markets in return for their social laws. As individualist as the other or as captive already to other races, the Western political elite and the Western economic elite both want more immigration, and much the same social laws.

A single world government can seem much like the days of European Empire, but our days of Empire were our races ruling over others for a common good. A single world government would be other races ruling over us for their particular good.

Accustomed as the West is to ruling the world, we presume world government would be our plaything to shape. It would not be. There are not enough white people on earth.

Most of the world does not want democracy, as we understand democracy. Those that do want democracy do not want the democracy that would empower other races to rule over them.

There is no international community. There is simply a self-serving Western elite, with a remarkably uniform world view. We are the only races subscribing.

Global self-determination is no self-determination. A parliament made up of the world's opinions imposed on all people would promptly eradicate the rights we hold dear. It might tax away the homes of those rich white people who enabled it or requisition those homes to be hostels or palaces for other races. There might never be a second earth-wide election, even if there happens to be a first. The only thing better for business than a single world government might be a single world government failing.

The Zionist Paradox

England expelled the Jews living there in 1290. France expelled the Jews there in 1306.

Having expelled her Muslim invaders following the completion of the Reconquista, Spain also evicted her Jewish intruders with the Alhambra Decree in 1492, if the Jews did not convert to Christianity. Those Jews returned to the lands of their ancestors: Israel and Judah.

Similarly in Portugal, King Manuel I in 1496 ordered all Jews to accept baptism as Christians or leave the country. In 1497, he converted all Jews in Portugal to Christians by royal decree. In 1499, he forbade them from leaving the country.

Many Portuguese suspected the so-called New Christians of continuing to practice Judaism, leading to outbreaks of violence. In 1506, with drought and a plague crippling Portugal, a New Christian in Lisbon mocked Portuguese talk of a miracle. Portuguese churchgoers killed him and an estimated nineteen hundred other New Christians in the ensuing riots, with Dominican friars urging people to "extinguish the wicked race." Portuguese also died.

Embarrassed by the failure of his efforts to integrate the Jews into Portuguese society, Manuel I executed two of those friars and approximately five hundred rioters. He stripped the City of Lisbon of important privileges. From 1507, he allowed the emigration of New Christians: Jews.

When Jews felt they could only be assured of justice in a Jewish country, as French Jews felt after the Dreyfus Affair in 1894 and '96, their eyes turned to that same ancient land. Zionism is Jewish self-determination: a Jewish homeland.

Since World War II, Jews and the West have followed two primary strategies in our determination to avert another Jewish Holocaust, at least one committed by white people. The first was eradicating white racism.

To that end, the West has multiracial immigration. Mixing with a handful of people from other races might make us sympathetic or antagonistic towards them. We need a lot of them to feel afraid.

Besides, with so many other races around us, we are less focused upon Jews. Anyone aspiring to cleanse our countries of other races has so many races through which to work, the Jews are unlikely to be the first to go, at least as far as white people are concerned.

The second strategy to avert another Jewish Holocaust was to create a place where Jews are safe: a Jewish homeland. In 1948, the modern state of Israel came into being.

The two strategies are contradictory: rejecting racial integrity for the West but defending it for Jews. It is absurd to reject the concept of race and thus nation for the West while maintaining there should be, or even could be, a racially Jewish state, but we do.

Israel's Law of Return in 1950 declared Israel the natural home of Jews the world over, irrespective of whether they or their known relatives were Israeli citizens. A 1970 amendment to the Law of Return extended the Jews' right to return to Israel to their spouses, children, and grandchildren, as well as their spouses' children and grandchildren.

Individual Jews might have never before set foot in Israel, but the right to return is a racial return to the land their ancestors left two thousand years earlier. Israel does not deny Jews entry for being atheists, although the 1950 Law of Return excludes Jews who voluntarily adopt another religion. In April 2008, the Supreme Court of Israel acknowledged that Jews who had not been religiously Jewish could not renounce Judaism. They could return.

Also entitled to live in Israel are converts to Judaism, although Jews debate what makes a person a convert to Judaism. Simply choosing to become a Jew, as another person might choose to become a Christian or any other religion, does not satisfy Jews, although it would satisfy the West.

There are limits. The Law of Return allows Israel to deny Jews citizenship if they are dangerous.

Israel allows non-Jews to live and work in Israel without offering them citizenship. Babies born in Israel can only get Israeli citizenship if at least one parent is a citizen. Non-Jewish permanent residents may only obtain Israeli citizenship upon conditions including them demonstrating their knowledge of Hebrew.

Racial integration is not always a Jewish vision, not even in the West. Wanting segregation without statehood, Orthodox Jews retain well-defined communities, separate from everyone else, wherever they live in the world. Orthodox Jews reject the notion of a Jewish state, Israel, until the messiah comes, even if they live there.

The Holocaust did not destroy the faiths of all Jews. For the Orthodox, it affirmed it. They see the *Shoah* as God's punishment for Jews having started to integrate with Gentiles in the decades beforehand. It became our punishment too.

Fortress Israel

With the state of Israel, Jews became less global. Jews built Israel from the sand and defend it from growing millions of Arabs and other Muslims wanting them gone. Open borders disempowering dominant races are for the homeless West, but not fortress Israel.

Much as white South Africans slowly ceased being able to rely on support from white people outside South Africa, so eventually did Jews. In our ideological hierarchy of victimhood since the Holocaust, the West defers to other races because we think they are all our victims, but we are not sure who to choose when they are at odds with each other.

Sometimes we lump Jews with the West in refusing them their self-determination; a thousand years and more in Europe will do that. Having removed Western borders, we are upset that Israel believes in its borders. Having decided to welcome everyone, eagerly becoming minorities in what were our cities and countries, we think Israel should too. We have no sympathy for Israel not welcoming a Muslim majority as we would. Arabs become victims of Jewish intolerance.

Other countries outside the West also enforce their borders.

They do not have millions of Arabs on their doorsteps wanting to enter.

Israel has accepted Ethiopian and other adherents to Judaism not racially Jewish, along with other refugees, but the numbers are tiny aside Western admissions. The numbers are big only in comparison with other countries outside the West.

Unlike Europeans, Jewish birth rates are highest where they are most under threat, but their rate in Israel remains less than the rates of other races there. Higher birth rates of immigrant races in the West than our birth rates do not bother us. Higher birth rates for Ethiopians than Jews in Israel bother some Jews. Some Jews took measures to curtail Ethiopian births.

Higher birth rates for Arabs in Israel bother Jews more. It is a demographic war, waged with babies. With enough Muslims in that rare Middle East democracy, Israel will eventually vote itself out of existence.

Anti-Zionism

Arab nationalism is not content with the many Arab states. Arabs living in Israel have more rights than in most, if not all, Arab states, but Arabs complain about life under democratically elected Jews rather than life in a land under Arab authority.

Established in 1994, the Palestinian Authority's first law made selling land to Jews a capital offence. Palestinian Arabs are not planning to accommodate minority Jews in their state, if they ever get it, as Israel has accommodated minority Arabs, or as the West accommodates both.

Disenfranchising Jews from the West would be unacceptable anti-Semitism. Disenfranchising Jews from Israel is more acceptable anti-Semitism. They too can all come to the West.

Opposing self-determination for Jews in their ancestral land while supporting Palestinian Arabs wanting that land, with so many states already Arab, can only be anti-Semitic. Anti-Zionism is socially acceptable anti-Semitism, especially for people denying their anti-Semitism.

The West does not equate Zionism with racism because we think only white people are racist. Muslims equate Zionism with racism and they are right, but Arab self-determination is equally racist. Across Africa, Asia, and the oceans are other racial states equally racist. A hundred million Arabs and other Muslims complain about Jewish (and white) racism, but do not acknowledge their racism. Neither do we.

Europeans (other than Germans) might frown upon Jewish Israel as we would never frown upon Jewish Antwerp. In our darker moments, we blame the loss of our countries upon Jews.

Just as denying the Jews a country is anti-Semitic, denying Britons our country is anti-British. Denying the Scots or Welsh their own countries, if that is what they want, would be anti-Scot or anti-Welsh, although an independent Scotland or Wales would not really be a country for Scots or Welsh if it was subject to immigration.

God might have given the Jews Israel. He did not give them the West. The Holocaust that gave Jews their homeland ultimately cost white people our homelands.

Xenophobia

Our coming world order is not proving as comfortable as we thought or were told it would be. Our lands without borders, or borders too porous, leave many of us fearful.

Nevertheless, we dismiss warnings about the possible consequences of declining white populations much as we dismissed warnings about immigration: for being racist. The insult second only to being called racist is being called xenophobic: the brand scolded into the flesh of people not enthusiastically wanting boundless more immigrants.

So much as questioning the alleged economic, social, or cultural benefits of immigration, wondering whether it was or still is a good idea after all, is symptomatic of xenophobia: a supposedly irrational fear of foreigners. So much as considering there might be risks of interracial immigration, let alone examining those risks, is xenophobia.

Paradoxically, we dismiss any attempt at rationally examining the costs and consequences of immigration for being supposedly irrational. Like the rest of our postmodern phobias, we deem rationality to be irrational.

Our innate human prejudices against outsiders have become

xenophobia, as if human nature were irrational. It is not.

We do not call people of other races xenophobes for not wanting immigration into their countries, even by people of their race. Xenophobia is like bigotry and racism. It is a politically constructed affliction only white people suffer.

Human nature is not just tribal and racist. It is so-called xenophobic.

All countries, right across the world, are premised not just upon race but upon recognition of the dangers to a people and culture that outsiders pose, intentionally and, perhaps, unwittingly. They are premised upon racism and so-called xenophobia.

Outside the West, there is almost no interracial immigration. There is very little intra-racial immigration. There is no xenophobia.

Europhobia refers not to an irrational fear of Europeans but to European resistance to the European Union superstate. Because that opposition comes from a defence of European countries and cultures from globalism, Europhobia is akin to xenophobia.

Immersed in our individualism, we think something is mentally wrong with white people caring about other white people. So-called xenophobia includes recognising the harm immigration inflicts upon our compatriots, even if not obviously upon us. In our individualist West, empathy and loyalty for our compatriots have become mental illness, as a lack of them is not.

Empathising with our race is racist. Empathising with other races would not be, if we ever really did.

There is no word for rationally questioning immigration, wondering whether our lives or our children's lives would be better without interracial immigration. So convinced are we of the glories of multiculturalism without having questioned it, we cannot imagine that any rational person would question it. Questioning immigration could only be irrational, we think.

Any contemplation that our countries are ours, our homes, is xenophobia. Presuming that all sane people want to do is earn money, spend money, and watch sport, we think white people valuing their race, culture, or country must be irrational. Thus any desire to save our races, countries, and cultures becomes irrational.

So confident are in other races and so hostile to our own, whatever the record of other races in their countries or in ours, we are certain that simply wondering whether we should fear rising numbers of other races must also be irrational. To fear the loss of our countries makes someone practically insane.

Racial and Religious Vilification

We see only goodness and merit in other races and their religions: those races and religions in which we found confidence after losing confidence in our own. Seeing badness or failing in other races or their religions, we call racial or religious vilification.

Seeing anything bad or inferior about white people or Christianity is not racial or religious vilification, not since the Holocaust. Racial or religious vilification is like racism and xenophobia. Only white people are guilty.

We are increasingly making racial or religious vilification a criminal offence. They are more arms of so-called hate speech.

Immigration being premised upon our great confidence in other races, questioning immigration is questioning that great confidence. Prohibiting racial or religious vilification thus stymies any rational assessment of immigration.

We see only the supposed benefits from immigration, but any rational assessment of immigration or anything else must also consider the costs. Explicit or implicit in considering those costs will be consideration of any possible faults or weaknesses in other races.

In a West unwilling to consider race rationally, anything less than our great confidence in other races becomes vilification, even if recognition of their faults or weaknesses is only in the context of them being in close proximity to us or to each other. Thus the faults or weaknesses might also be ours. They might be human nature.

We are thus supposed not to contemplate the consequences of immigration, not rationally at any rate. Questioning immigration is not just racist. It is racial or religious vilification.

Racial or religious vilification becomes akin to xenophobia. Implicit in any fear of other races and their religions is questioning their supposed kindness and good nature. If xenophobia is presumed to be irrational, then racial or religious vilification is presumed to be nasty: more bad than mad.

Prohibiting racial or religious vilification protects people of other races and their religions from any sort of review, rational or not. It shuts down discussion of possible links between race or religion and crime, terror, or anything else undesirable, even simple social breakdown, unless we want to refute it.

Thus it empowers other races to act without fear of consequence, even merely to their racial or religious reputation, however lazy, stupid, or wicked they are. Their community leaders have no need to discipline them, when we refuse to acknowledge their failings.

Their increasing numbers can only increase their power, especially when they are already powerful. Thus the power of the most powerful among them grows.

While we freely complain about powerful white people ruling over us, we are not supposed to contemplate another race or league of races ruling over us. If we do contemplate it, we are supposed to welcome the idea.

Not to welcome other races ruling over us would be to consider that something about other races is less than magnanimous. It becomes racial or religious vilification.

We shut down white people questioning what we are doing to us and to our descendants. We rebuke anyone suggesting we should deny other races their chances to become dominant majority populations over us. We torment our people who fear our racial decline.

Immigrants torment those white people too, but they are being loyal to their racial or religious interests as we are being hostile to ours. The futures of the West and Western races, cultures, and countries are not open for discussion, unless we welcome our decline.

Were other races on earth under siege but forbidden from mentioning it, they could enter the West claiming asylum. We have nowhere to go.

Race and Values

We are not proud of our liberal democracy, justice, and respect for human rights, let alone of taking them to the world, because we insist they are not ours. They are ours. The West created classic liberalism. It is more Western thought.

Our passions for personal freedoms are not shared by most of the world. The freedoms on which we predicate our lives are neither universal nor inalienable. They are too precious for that. We have human capacities, like thinking and speaking, but not even they are universal or inalienable.

Our presumption that other races desire our democracies underlies much of our immigration and foreign policies since World War II. We presume we are not imposing liberalism. We are releasing it.

Differences between countries we attribute to political and economic conditions, as we attribute everything to political and economic conditions, in spite of the blatant differences between Western countries and other rich democratic countries. We refuse to link differences in values and other facets of culture to race or religion as other races link them and as we used to link them, because we refuse to link anything to race or religion, except to malign our own.

We think our values are universal, because we think people are universal, but people are not universal. There are no universal values, as ought to be self-evident from even the most cursory examination of different countries around the world and different people within countries. Other races' values are not bad for being different, but they are not our values.

The West thinks freedom means the rights of the one, and all ones at that. Other races see freedom as the rights of the many: their many. We grant individual rights to people who are not individualistic.

Principles underpinning social systems underpin legal systems. We grant not just rights that other races do not grant, but access to courts and recourse to financial assistance they do not grant.

The very presumption of values being universal is a peculiarly Western presumption, although we recognise different values when it is a chance to commend other races and think less of ours. The values we know are not universal are their values better than ours.

Immigrants do not come to copy our values. They come because of our values, accommodating them and their values.

There is no reason in reality why people pursuing admission into the West should adopt Western values because we think they already hold them. There is even less reason their children should.

Besides, Western freedoms give immigrants the right not to

adopt our values. Multiculturalism expects them not to adopt our values.

When we believed in our nations and races, Europeans developed classic liberalism for sensing the betterment it brought our nations and races. Holding fast to any principle when it is harming our race and nation is not liberalism. It is ideology.

The End of Liberalism

Ours are the rights we do not demand be inalienable. We think they already are.

They are not. No rights are inalienable. They depend upon enough people wanting them and being able and willing to fight to defend them.

Values lie inside people's heads. Without people to believe them, values cease to exist.

Without countries to practice them, values are just words. They endure only until the last paper on which they are written rots away, the last stone tablet crumbles.

Abraham Lincoln understood as much when he went to war to hold the United States of America together. He was not willing to sacrifice America in his opposition to slavery, even if he inadvertently did.

We are willing to sacrifice the West, our cultures and civilisation, in our resolute opposition to racism and religious discrimination. Uninterested in Western liberalism, immigrants have not proven as tolerant of the West as the West is tolerant of immigrants, but in the name of tolerance, the West welcomes the intolerant. Intolerance spreads.

Only of white people's intolerance are we intolerant. Only the dissidents among us are intolerant of the intolerant among other races and their religions.

No country can remain liberal accommodating people opposed to liberalism, but we individuals do not mind if no countries continue reflecting our values provided we remain true to our values, in our shrinking little circles of good-hearted friends. We think we do not need countries, because we have our ideals to keep us.

Presuming that any of our liberties and institutions will remain as we become declining minorities in our countries is presumptuous, if not ludicrous. We simply cannot assume we will be free to live by our values as we become smaller parts of our national populations. Multicultural liberalism is our new Western ideal to which we hold fast, but changing demography means it will eventually vote itself out of existence.

That we no longer forge our countries in our image is no reason for other races not to forge what were our countries in their images. Democratic rights that we espouse so passionately entitle them to choose the systems by which they live.

Denying the new majorities the rights to make changes they believe to be right would be undemocratic. Our ideologies of choice will not begrudge them the right to impose their thinking and ways. Demographic democracy entitles them to live by their values, demanding we do so too if they wish. The very values that opened our countries to others might be the first values to fall.

The West equates freedom and equality with multiculturalism, as if the rest of the world is not free or equal and as if we were not free and equal before immigrants came. We have tied in our minds Western freedoms to giving our freedoms to other races. Our predecessors did not. Other races do not.

In fact, Western freedoms do not depend upon us giving them to other races. They depend upon us not giving them to other races, if giving them Western freedoms means them living in our countries.

A people are only free when they keep at bay those who would deny them their freedom. If we truly treasured freedom and rights, we would reject racial and religious diversity. We would enforce our borders from those who do not share our senses of liberty. No other races share our senses of liberty precisely, much as we do not share their senses of liberty precisely.

If we truly treasured freedom and rights, liberalism would again discriminate by race and religion. Liberalism would again be nationalistic. We would end interracial immigration.

Treason

From the French Revolution beginning in 1789, talk of political Left and Right arose, but both Left and Right remained fundamentally nationalistic. The crime for which the new regime executed King Louis XVI in 1793 was high treason.

The West no longer has nationalism but our nations endure, to a point, a little better than our empires endure. We insist that we are individuals of virtue, we citizens of the world, but we fake our oaths to our countries in those rare cases we are called upon to make oaths. Sincerity in our oaths to our countries would be nationalism.

It beggars belief to imagine immigrants are sincere with their oaths to our countries when we are insincere with our oaths, but we presume citizenship commands devotion to our countries from immigrants we do not feel ourselves. We are cavalier about our commitments to each other, but blithely assume immigrants will honour their commitments to us they make when they apply for our citizenship.

Besides, the children of immigrants make no pledges. With no more evidence than their community spokespeople speaking at microphones, we think immigrants are loyal to our countries to which we are no longer loyal. We are the ones who opened our borders. Why would immigrants defend our countries we do not?

White people with no patriotic feeling are nevertheless appalled at any suggestion that immigrants are not patriotic. It is another absurdity to which we are driven by our manic rejection of Western racism and nationalism.

There will hardly be patriotic others, when there are so few patriotic us. Perhaps all we expect of other races is that they love their races as much as we love them.

We feel no loyalty to the lands of our forebears. That is no reason to expect other races not to feel loyalty to the lands of their forebears.

We respect them retaining their histories and ancestries, while we incongruously assume they are not loyal to those histories and ancestries. Suspecting otherwise would be racist.

We presume immigrants cannot have been loyal to their ancestral lands to have left those ancestral lands, but that disregards the incentives we give them to come and to stay and it disregards the benefits they remit to their homelands from ours. People patriotic to their ancestral homelands are not offering patriotism to their countries of residence or even countries of citizenship, if the two ever conflict.

They are often not offering patriotism to our countries even if the two never conflict. We are not.

Living in the West and even citizenship of Western countries do not lead us to be loyal to our races and countries. Nor does living in the West or citizenship of Western countries diminish other races' loyalties to their races and countries: their ancestral homelands. The most it might do is inspire in those immigrants a little layer of loyalty to our countries above any regard they might have for other countries because that loyalty is in their interests, but they still offer nothing at odds with their loyalty to their ancestral homelands.

We have moved beyond individualism to counter-nationalism. More than simply discarding our national interests, we actively oppose our national interests, when it suits us. Treason no longer offends the West. It is a right.

In our dedication to multiculturalism, treason is practically an obligation, as we once recognised treason to be. Ridiculous it might be, but having redefined Western countries to be multicultural, multiculturalism becomes patriotism. Globalism, the erasure of those same countries, becomes patriotism. For resisting multiculturalism and interracial immigration, multiculturalist ideology denotes what was formerly patriotism to be sedition, for loving our countries and cultures.

While other races co-operate, we betray. Western businesspeople cuddling up to foreigners for a few more pieces of silver express the same contempt for their countries and cultures as their spouses and children carrying placards welcoming refugees. We betray each other, but expect immigrants not to betray us too.

Modern-Day Empires

Some of the boundaries we now see between countries, our forebears set between our empires. Those countries' borders upon independence were the product of past European imperialism.

Other boundaries we now see between countries, other races' forebears set between their empires. Those borders are products of other races' imperialism.

We do not mind imperialism, when it is other people's empires. We condemn past European imperialism, while condoning not just other races' past imperialism, but their present imperialism too. We only fear white people.

Other races' empires are not of ideology as ours have become. Their empires are of race, culture, and nation, often where ours used to be. With self-belief we have lost, the rest of the world feels none of the shame for its past and present colonisations that we feel for our past colonisation.

While the West's obsession with economic growth drives immigration, Asian economic imperialism fosters emigration, temporarily or permanently. Commercial colonialism comes without sense of bringing civilisation, real or imagined. It is simply earning money and otherwise acquiring wealth, much as it did with past Asian emigration into Europe's empires of old. It can also mean spending money.

We do not like pessimism. We see merit in optimism. Our vision of a world without borders is predicated upon our unwavering confidence in the kindness of other races, as we do not imagine in our forebears when the empires were ours.

Reverse Colonisation

When we settled in other countries, we called it colonialism. When other races settle in our countries, we call it immigration.

Without us asserting our sovereignty, our countries ceased being rivals of other races. They became opportunities.

We made our countries lands for the world. We made them available. Our abodes became beacons for all races wanting better lives, whatever the impact upon us.

The West having lost our self-belief, our sense of what constitutes civilisation came to be not our civilisation or civilisations, but everyone else's civilisations. No longer colonising the world to spread civilisation, we came to imagine other races colonising our countries to civilise us, whatever they think or do.

The conclusion of our colonisation of the world became the start of the world's colonisation of us. In our gleeful surrender, we welcome the new colonisations as we no longer cherish our old. We are the willing white minorities.

Reverse colonialism turns the old colonialism back to front. Through our age of empires, Western countries were microcosms for what we thought the planet should be. They still are, but we are no longer transforming the world in our image. We are transforming the West in the world's image.

By refusing to treat our countries as ours, we invite other races to treat our countries as theirs. What had been geographically the West became open for other races building empires of their own.

There was a time we called people xenophobic for warning that we would lose our countries to immigration. We came to call people xenophobic for saying we have not lost our countries to immigration: that our countries are still ours.

We are passing through diversity into something else. What had been a bloc of Western Civilisation across Europe, parts of the Americas, Australasia, and patches elsewhere become bits of other people's blocs.

We do not have a bloc anymore. We are individuals.

Our individualism allows other races' expansion. We have left lacunas where our countries were.

Racial connections remain, connecting Western countries more to those countries from which immigrants come than to each other. When we are looking for affinity between our cities or countries, it is no longer based upon our common race. It is based upon another common race replacing us in both.

When other races possess the lands that we give them, they will defend them for their descendants as we refuse to defend our lands for ours. They do now of the lands they possess, however they acquired them.

Imperial China

While Beijing insists that Taiwan is part of China, Taiwan's indigenous population is not racially Chinese. Increasing Chinese colonisation of the island from the seventeenth century, and especially after the Allied Powers delivered administration to China from Japan after World War II, overwhelmed the indigenous Taiwanese population. In 1947, China massacred tens of thousands of Taiwanese protesters in Taipei.

In 1951, while Europeans were withdrawing from our colonies and before we began apologising tirelessly for having been there, China took control of Tibet, formally annexing it in 1959. Gauging public opinion in China at the time is difficult, but there was no audible protest from Chinese people outside China. Chinese colonisation subsequently diluted Tibetan culture, with the most credible estimates of Tibetan casualties in the order of two hundred thousand killed and injured.

In April 2008, the Chinese government killed Tibetans protesting against Chinese rule. Without talk of diversity being their strength or celebrations of multiculturalism, the Chinese government promised to step up the re-education of Tibetans to become loyal to China.

Tibetans around the world and many white people condemned the killings. We protested against the Chinese government, but not China or Chinese people as we protest against white people.

Defending their country's reputation, thousands of Chinese outside China (including those with Western citizenship) abused Tibetan and Western protesters. Whatever the conflicts between them, Chinese people and their governments stand together in conflicts with people of other races, with racial loyalty undivided by nationality.

Consumed by politics but refusing to confront issues of race, the West mutedly complains of the Chinese Communist Party while pointedly embracing Chinese people. That is not a distinction we make in blaming Germany and Germans for the crimes of the Nazi Party. Neither do Germans.

Chinese people make that distinction between themselves. Their dealings with outsiders can appear more problematic, but Chinese and other races have long drawn upon outside assistance to assist them in their internecine conflicts. Like other races, but unlike ours, Chinese people only side with other races against people of their race in their sectional interests.

The Western citizenships we often trivialise within our countries we expect other countries to respect when our citizens are there, but while we identify immigrants purely by their citizenship, countries outside the West do not. Chinese people remain, in effect, Chinese nationals in spite of Western citizenship.

China divides the people of the world into Chinese, overseas Chinese, and foreigners. The great-great-grandchildren of émigrés who cannot speak Chinese are not foreigners in China. They are overseas Chinese. People of other races born in Chinese territory remain foreigners, however fluent their Chinese might be.

China lauds Chinese people bringing capital, technology, and foreign contact to Mother China as *tong bao* (compatriots), whatever their citizenship. Those Chinese are content remaining Chinese, only citing their foreign citizenship when they fall afoul of Chinese authorities and they expect those foreign countries to help them. Their interest is theirs, not ours.

The converse to the Chinese receiving loyalty from fellow Chinese in spite of their foreign citizenship is the loyalty those Chinese grant them. The Chinese government intervenes to protect Chinese people overseas, including those foreign born whose families have been away from China for generations.

While China might extradite foreigners charged with crimes to other countries, China does not extradite its nationals. China, if not necessarily Hong Kong, is the Chinese diaspora's refuge from Western laws.

Europe is not our refuge from anything. That would be racist.

China does not import workers. It trains its people. We train them too.

The Chinese government does not just teach children in China. It teaches children in the West, and not only Chinese. The Chinese are taking advantage of the West's multiculturalism to spread out, while preventing information and ideas from flowing back to contaminate China.

Like other countries outside the West, there is no immigration into China like that into the West. The only refugees China has allowed to settle there have been fellow Chinese fleeing Vietnam from 1979 to '82 due to conflict between the two countries, along with a tiny number of Vietnamese travelling with them. Those Vietnamese number no more than two percent of the total number of refugees China admitted.

Four decades onward, China still denies those Chinese and Vietnamese refugees citizenship. China expects them someday to return to Vietnam.

Birth Control

Increasingly embracing other races, refusing to distinguish our race from others, the West began fearing a worldwide population explosion through the 1960s. We retreated from procreation to sustainability.

In time, we retreated still further. Our visions of the world do not just allow us to be childless. They require it.

Crowded countries in Asia reduced their childbearing for the sake of their nations. Refusing racial identities creates the same impetus in us.

Other races consider their countries. We consider the world.

Our sense of inclusion means the population pressures we sense are not ours. The abundance of other people's children leaves us feeling too many people are already on earth, persuading us not to bear children. We do not want other white people to bear them.

We compare rates of birth and death across the globe and produce graphs of a growing population, oblivious to our people aging and populations falling. Confusing populations with people and refusing to recognise race, we rarely talk about our dearth of white babies. It is no longer news.

We care for the sustainability of the natural environment, much as we care for the sustainability of other races and their families. We do not care about the sustainability of our races and families. That would be racist.

We fear the effects of excess population as if all people were the same. We do not acknowledge that the world already has the capacity to feed, clothe, and shelter everyone. Nor do we acknowledge that, with Western industry, technology, and especially charity, we do more to feed, clothe, and shelter people than other races do.

Good policy differs between different peoples, places, and periods. In some poor countries, their paramount human rights have been alleviating poverty by curtailing birth rates, even if that necessitated restricting individual rights to bear children.

If the West really wanted to better the world instead of feeling wonderful about throwing time and money at other races in aid, we would cut birth rates across the poor crowded countries that will never support themselves. Instead, we complain about countries outside the West mandating birth control.

Meanwhile, we complain about Western countries restricting birth control. The only population we control is our free-living own.

Anti-abortion campaigners in America complain more about black women than white women aborting their babies. We hate racism so much.

They protest the 1973 Supreme Court decision in *Roe v Wade*, which gave poor women the legal rights to abortion that rich women do not need. Rich women use contraception, and are more likely to obtain safe abortions whatever their legal rights. Poor women have abortions, depending upon public clinics. Poor people are disproportionately black.

Roe v Wade saved America from millions of unwanted poor babies. They would have grown up without fathers, or without families at all, often to become criminals.

Government Assistance

Valuing their races, the peoples of the world persevere. Those people so assured in their races and cultures are growing.

If they are not growing, like Japan and Korea, they are keeping their countries to replenish someday. They are even emigrating to Western countries, without disappearing at the rates we are.

Japanese, Korean, and other governments outside the West respond to their low birth rates with measures to encourage marriage and increase birth rates among their people. Not us.

Western government assistance to parents does not seek to increase our birth rates. It generally does not distinguish between giving birth and adoption, even foreign adoption.

Only in the unnatural West do we presume that children need money more than they need parents or step-parents, or at least that the parents or guardians need money. Western government subsidies favouring single parents discourage them from marrying.

Nor does Western government assistance generally distinguish between races, and certainly never to favour ours. It might favour indigenous races, unless we are the indigenous race.

We imagine rights to almost everything, but draw the line at a right to bearing a child. We just open the immigration valve wider.

Western interests are immediate; we do not want to wait. Immigrants with families already in place and adoptions bring new generations into the fold much sooner than waiting nine or more months for pregnancies to bear consumers. Population growth in Western countries has come to be entirely due to immigration, including immigrants already come, and old people living longer.

Immigration does not redress our appallingly low birth rates. It exacerbates them.

Populations naturally stabilise. High birth rates create crowding, which dissuades people from bearing children.

Immigration also causes crowding, which further depresses our birth rates. Immigration demands more immigration.

Conversely, low birth rates create space, until the awareness of a dwindling population encourages births, among people who care. We lose that opportunity because of immigration.

Meanwhile, the countries from which immigrants come to the West are spared incentives to reduce their birth rates. Their emigration is a release valve, deferring the population pressures that might have curtailed their births. It cannot continue forever, but only until the West drowns in their global overflows.

Racial Replacement

We in the West are told not to bear children because the world is over-populated. On the other hand, we are told we must accept migrants because we do not bear children.

Other races see their generation's role being to prepare succeeding generations. So do we, but not our succeeding generations. We invite other races to replace us.

Western interests are individual. Immigrants' interests are also those of their families and race. They come to craft better lives for them and their children, as we no longer imagine for us and ours. We share what we have with other races, rather than keeping what we have for our children.

The open West is very different for immigrants than white people. They are gaining countries. We are losing ours.

Life is harder now than it was a generation or two ago. It is harder because we are giving away our inheritance and our children's inheritance. We advance other races at our and our children's expense.

We do not discriminate to save our sacrificial children, let alone our compatriots' children. Defending them would be xenophobic. Abandoning our children for other races' children we think is inclusive.

No amount of ideology, marketing, or macroeconomic data

conceals from the West our fear the future will be worse than the present. Becoming minorities in our cities and countries makes white people's futures too insecure for us to be parents. Knowing our children will live lesser lives than ours, we have no yearning to bring them into countries we feel helpless to retain.

Above all other reasons for our fewer births, it is the saddest and most telling, distinguishing the West's fallen birth rates from those in rich crowded Asian countries. Other races expect their futures to be better than the present, their children to live better lives than theirs. Feeling their futures are within their control, their peoples are on their sides.

Our despair compounds. With so few of our children, our lives will be worse. So we have fewer children.

We do all we can for other people's children. We are not so concerned for our own.

Among the hardest aspects of Western parenting is knowing that nobody cares. Caring only adds to our despair.

We are the perfects hosts. Our challenge is not to preserve our people, but to house and school immigrants before we die, bequeathing our lands to them.

Our sense of a single people and planet supersedes Western streets, suburbs, and countries: a planet without us. Amidst the billions of people on earth, we without race do not realise we are dying. We might be changing, but we do not notice the change. Losing our homelands means losing our races.

Replacing one race with another race or with other races replaces the culture of that race with the culture or cultures of that other race or races. What had been our economy becomes their economy, while our people can die without our deaths appearing in the national accounts.

Dispossession

We are not so willing to describe our countries as being ours anymore. Instead, immigrants declare our countries to be theirs: that they take the countries we give them.

Their countries of origin are their countries too. Refusing to recognise race, we cannot see their two countries any more than we can see our one country.

We alone opened our countries to other races, to the point of losing what we had. While we weep for other races having been subsumed, we welcome other races subsuming us.

The fewer white people, we are told the more cosmopolitan a country. It is an approach premised upon unabashed hostility to white people. All those racially homogenous countries without any white people become very cosmopolitan.

If so much of our lives can be driven by the loss of our family homes, then so much more can be driven by the loss of our national homes. Much like our indigenous peoples, white people have not gone anywhere, but we are feeling like intruders to the lands in which we, our parents, and our grandparents were born. We have become strangers, but when those left alone do not celebrate their aloneness, we throw them further aside.

We offer our race none of the sympathy we afford other races. It is hard to know what more Western governments or people could have done to welcome immigrants, but still we sympathise for immigrants feeling unwelcome in the West, although they voluntarily undertook the changes in their lives, improving their lives, and in their new homes are in growing communities.

When indigenous races feel demoted by colonial races, we are so quick to care, unless we are the indigenous race. We commiserate, even cry, for other indigenous people feeling pains of dispossession from the lands of their birth. We mock white people feeling the same, feeling dispossessed from the nations their forebears founded, built, and defended, but that we have not defended as our forebears defended. White people suffering dispossession because of immigration get no understanding.

They are white folk: a relatively mild epithet aside other epithets thrown against white people, but still a pejorative way to describe people of our race. We mention them to malign them for not welcoming the loss of their countries, cultures, and civilisation: for retaining belief they ever had countries, cultures, and civilisation to begin with or that their countries, cultures, and civilisation were ever worth keeping. They are the malcontents reticent about becoming racial minorities and even about their race disappearing altogether, who contemplate any negativity about it. They are old-fashioned, stupid, unable to cope.

We demand understanding for other races' experiences, but do not try to comprehend our compatriots' fears. We do not imagine the lives they have lived: their nationalism giving them ownership of nations their governments stripped from them, without their choosing, without them having a say. We torment people of our race feeling disenfranchised from the only homes they and their forebears have known.

Western countries are no longer homes for our races. The West is no longer home for white people.

To be a postmodern white person is to be buffeted back and forth, unwanted outside the West and within, without anywhere to feel secure. Denying people their innate desires to live among their kind in a land of their own would be oppression, unless we are the people.

At some point, the propagandists for immigration proceed from denying that something will happen or is happening because of immigration, to celebrating that it is happening or has happened. Playing out vividly before us is the end of our futures, but when torrents of immigrants test the West's willingness to give up our countries, cultures, and races, we cry out that we are!

A Land of our Own

By the standards of the world, the West is strikingly nice. Open doors to our countries are open doors to our premises. Neither countries nor private functions are ours. We can hardly blame immigrants for thinking our houses are similarly open.

We need boundaries for our well-being, peace of mind, and fulfilment. We need sometimes to say "No."

We understand personal property so well when it comes to the cars we drive, houses in which we reside, and beds in which we sleep. Private ownership motivates people. Private landholdings secure us. We understand ownership of our homes better than we understand ownership of our homelands.

Wanting a country to own is not fear or loathing, prejudice or bigotry. We can like all the people and places on earth, but still need countries of some kind.

White people wanting our countries back do not hate other races. We simply do not hate our own.

With our countries, we had our place in the world. Without countries, we have no place in the world.

Every time we think globally, we are left ultimately to think solitarily. Without nationalism, we are each of us narrowed to solitude.

Among the people wanting countries in which to belong are many of us doing personally well. We simply feel what other races feel: collective connections to the lands of our forebears and birth, to countries that our forebears forged and died to defend. We honour our ancestors, as people of other races honour theirs. We care for our descendants and race, racist that might be, rather than succumbing to Western individualism.

Other races do not insult us by not letting us live in their lands. We would not insult them if we did the same. Other races would not tolerate being replaced in their countries.

If we really believed all races are the same, in some primeval, instinctive ways, we would see in ourselves what we respect in others: our yearning for a collective connection to country. We would want countries as other races and ethnic groups want or enjoy. We would want a continent or large portion of one, or a patch of ocean and islands, as other races want or enjoy. We would want blocs of earth.

Some part of all of us (poorly neglected of late) yearns to be a people in a country around us. Our yearning might be unrequited, but it is yearning nevertheless.

Bilateral Immigration

We are still giving rights to the rest of the world, welcoming other races, even when our lives are not so good anymore. When white people question immigration, we do not materially change our policies. We change our people.

Were Western governments representing their people, they would alleviate their anxieties. That would be nationalism.

If we are not so bold as to dream of recovering our countries and continent completely, then we can at least stop our circumstances worsening. Bilateral immigration would be us admitting immigrants only from countries admitting the same numbers and natures of immigrants from us.

We could stop beckoning people to come with jobs our compatriots could do, welfare benefits, or anything else. We could prohibit trespass.

We could do what the rest of the world does. Instead of granting foreigners rights of residence, we might grant them permits to remain, provided our people do not suffer as a result. Their permission to stay in our countries might be nominally permanent, through the rest of their lives, but always with the caveat we can withdraw that permission if our compatriots' and national interest require it. Our compatriots' interest is our national interest. That is nationalism.

We would pay them wages and salaries for work they performed, but not pay them welfare or pensions. We would not pay or subsidise the costs of their healthcare, children's education, or anything else. Aside perhaps from a few specific categories of resident applicants or noteworthy individuals, we would not offer them or their children citizenship.

The permission we grant, we would grant only the good. From the bad or possibly bad, we would revoke their permission to stay.

We do not expect other races to sacrifice or suffer for our benefit. Why must our compatriots and descendants sacrifice or suffer for their benefit?

Generous as we are, we might grant our friends refuge, but only refuge and only for as long as they need it. If people visit our home and forever sit in our sofas, eat from our kitchens, and sleep in our beds, generation after generation, then it is no longer our home.

We fail to distinguish individuals from groups, as other races do. We do not appreciate the possibility of restricting citizenship to our race, while allowing our friends from other races but only our friends to live with us.

Diasporas

Speaking of the Jewish diaspora has fallen from favour, but diaspora it is: the original Diaspora. Their ancestral homeland is Israel, from which all racial Jews came.

A diaspora means more than people dispersing from their homeland. It is a continuing sense of collective identity long after they dispersed: a cogent, biological wholeness encompassing them, their generations passed, and their generations to come.

Their diaspora links all people of an ethnic group or race to their ancient homeland wherever they are, bringing them peace of mind and self-respect. Their ancient homeland is no less their ancestral home if they have never been there. However long ago their ancestors departed and however many countries they have subsequently traversed, they enjoy and suffer their diaspora.

Diasporas connect people culturally, politically, and economically. They mean most when people of a race are attacked, or even just mocked. They mean almost as much when people of their race are attacking others, or even just mocking others.

From Europe, we children of empires came, shining with our British and other European diasporas. Europe's children explored the world with our homelands and all of Europe at our backs, but diasporas are racial. We have felt less and less of our diasporas since two world wars we so painfully won and more painfully lost.

We no longer explore. Our ancestral homelands and the rest of Europe are no longer at our backs.

The West lost our senses of diaspora. We have become individuals, associating ourselves with our ancestral homelands no more than with Timbuktu.

We might even associate ourselves more with Timbuktu. We think the Malians need us.

Reunifying our Diasporas

In the 1960s, Malcolm X believed that American Negroes could recover their peace of mind and self-respect by identifying with Africa: by being African Americans. He sought to unify the African diaspora.

In our individualist West, the adjectives by which we call people African Americans and so forth are not supposed to be racial descriptors, because we no longer believe in race. They are geographical, ancestral pasts, but we descendants of those who left Europe do not call ourselves European. Our ancestors do not matter.

The Anglosphere simply speaks English. French Canadians are not Canadian French, but French-speaking Canadians. It is a matter of language, not ancestry.

Nor do we call those of us living in Africa or Asia, Africans or Asians. We are whites, as blacks and browns sometimes still are but reds and yellows never still are.

We are Caucasians, as Negroes and Mongoloids no longer are, but not from any last reverence for science in our treatment of race. Nor are we claiming ancestral links to the Caucasus between Europe and Asia. We are simply grappling for a word akin to race other than being European. We are people without ancestry.

Europe becomes just a place. We treat being European as living there. Non-Europeans are not living there. We want to ensure immigrants to Europe feel no less European for having forebears from somewhere else.

If descendants of ancient European peoples allowed in ourselves what we respect in people of other races, we would again feel our diasporas. We would be what we are, wherever we are.

Europe's sometimes wayward children dispersed through the rest of the world would again be European. Other races would not be European, not even in Europe, much as we are not African in Africa or Asian in Asia.

We would look upon our ancestral homelands as other races look upon their ancestral homelands, however many generations ago we left. Not just Europe but the particular homelands of our ancestors would be our homelands too: Britain, Ireland, and so forth.

We would rediscover Europe and her colonies: the West. Were we to take other races' lead, we would reunify our diasporas.

The West does not cease being European, because we think we have ceased. We are Western or European if our ancestors came from Europe. Other races are not.

Where we were born does not matter. Nor does it matter, for these purposes, whether we live in Europe or elsewhere. We are no less European for being colonial European, no less British for being children of Empire.

Indigenous Europeans

If we become a bit envious of our friends from immigrant races, then it is not only because we assure them that what was our land is theirs. It is because they retain their ancestral lands, back home in Asia, Africa, or the oceans. Moving around the world, they can hark back to their homelands behind them they might never see.

They need not live there to know their countries, races, and cultures endure. The borderless West can collapse but Koreans in Kentucky know Korea is safe.

Most of those homelands are racially homogenous. Those that are not racially homogenous leave no doubt that their ancient peoples predominate.

Those immigrants can care for their ancestral homelands, knowing those ancestral homelands care more about them than about anyone else beyond their borders, wherever they happen to be. They, including the people we regard as being refugees, normally have choice where they live between Western countries and those ancestral homelands, however much we like to think otherwise.

If we have something to give and for as long as we give it, those homelands might let us reside there, for a time. Otherwise, we have only the West, or part of it, in which to live. We belong nowhere else.

If colonial Europeans' homelands cannot be the lands in which we were born, because we defer so completely to the indigenous races, then it is the land from which our forebears sailed. Europe is the Europeans' ancestral continent, whether we live there or not. Within Europe, we have our particular ancestral lands and islands.

Europe's colonial sons and daughters visit our ancestral lands as foreigners, confined to long queues at airports, ferry terminals, and railway stations. Hurried ahead of us are people whose passports make them European, as we are deemed not to be; Western countries discriminate on the basis of passports, to a point. We are the homeless colonials, Mother Europe's bastard children, who do not belong in Europe anymore. Our mother countries abandoned us after World War II, while we ran away.

Without Europe to call ours, similarly unable to call Europe theirs are the people in Europe racially European: Europeans who never left. There, we are the indigenous peoples, but indigenous identity is selective: an eminence we do not offer ourselves.

While we submit to indigenous races where we are not indigenous, where we are the indigenous people, we have rejected the concept. Being indigenous means being in a place before Europeans came.

Only white people can be racist and xenophobic. Only white people cannot be indigenous.

We are the only races to whom we do not recognise indigenous rights. Those of us who remained in Europe get no particular recognition, no special status in our ancient homes. No host or hostess begins a school, cultural, or other public gathering in Europe by acknowledging and respecting the traditional owners and custodians of the land, their elders past and present, as we tirelessly do at public gatherings, even university lectures, in Australia in deference to Aborigines.

In Australia, we defer to the local Aboriginal tribe by name. We do so without having met any of the tribespeople and often without having met any Aborigines.

In Europe, we could do the same of the local European tribe. In England, those traditional owners and custodians of the land, their elders past and present, are the English. In Scotland, Wales, and Ireland, they are the Scots, Welsh, and Irish, and so forth.

A European Home

In 1968, the Commonwealth Immigrants Bill granted a limited right of return to people whose parents or grandparents had left Britain. The British right to return, such as it is, vests only in the children and grandchildren of British citizens. It was expressly not racial but national, as being British had officially become.

Europe's rights of return are matters of law. They are rights to live and work in places without presumption our hearts are there. White people are not supposed to love our lands anymore, not as our lands.

Sometimes, far from the eyes and ears of the mob, in small government offices among lowly government staff, we breathe a little. We quietly welcome our race, as people of other races publicly welcome theirs.

Other indigenous races' enjoy preferential rights to their ancestral homelands. Lebanon granted Lebanese a right of return, when they needed it from Brazil.

Europe could respond to our low birth rates by allowing all her treasured offspring to return: to be as welcoming of our prodigal peoples as we have become welcoming of everyone else. We would again be her sons and daughters, with colonial Europeans returning home to repopulate any number of generations after we left to populate our colonies.

We would be ancestral Europeans in our ancient lands, if our ancient lands allow us. Ours would be discrimination with courtesy, in favour of our own.

The motherlands that Europe once shared with her faraway children, she revoked. She can revoke what she offered the rest.

If our past imperialism condemns the Americas and Australasia to being multiracial elsewhere, then it need not condemn Europe. For those of us remaining in our colonies, the conflicts and crises of multiculturalism would be easier to bear with our ancestral homes and heritage intact, our future secure, as they are for immigrants. We could be at the far side of the earth never touching lush European soil, but not fret so much for the New World we are losing to know the Old World endures.

Africa for the Africans was a theme through our withdrawal from Africa following World War II. If we should have left our lands of empire because they were not our ancestral lands, then other races should leave Europe. If European races do not belong outside Europe, then other races do not belong in Europe: Europe for the Europeans. Without Europeans in Europe, we are not anywhere, while gypsy strangers take our place in the Pyrenees.

2. THE FAILURE
OF MULTICULTURALISM

When we of the West had community, unity, and strength, we did not need banners telling us we had community, unity, and strength. We had no need to declare we were happy, when we really were happy. Not trying so hard to convince ourselves that the present was wonderful, our forebears felt no need to denigrate our past.

Rather than rules demanding that students celebrate diversity around school classroom walls, there were multiplication tables. Children learnt little things like reading, writing, and arithmetic. Rather than posters telling children who they must respect, children decided for themselves who they respected.

Our British and other Western societies we have come to despise worked well, the best ordered societies on earth. If we did not lose faith in them through two world wars and a holocaust, we came to take them for granted.

Young people do not know what they are missing because of multiculturalism and diversity, because we tell them they are not missing anything. Older people telling us their olden-day memories could teach us the past, but we too rarely ask and even more rarely listen. When people who were there speak of the past, we do not hear their elderly memories.

Old people can be so negative about the changes they have seen. When old people tell us how much better our lives were before other races came, we dismiss them for being racist. Our relentless devotion to multiculturalism commands that we insist our lives are better for other races coming, in spite of the truth. It commands we scrap our Western past.

Western Etiquette

We presume that people are so much the same, but people's values reflect the values of their races in which they were raised.

Behaviours that some communities consider to be good others consider to be bad. Morals depend much upon tribe, race, and religion.

Our traditional British and other Western standards were not those of other races. They did not contribute to us forming them. If our manners and mores we shared were not what we did, then they were what we knew we should do.

When we had self-belief, we inspired some people of other races to practice our courtesies and etiquette in our countries and in theirs, but we have lost our self-belief. They feel no obligation to practice them, not even in our countries. Without us requiring them to do so, they do not.

There is no reason why people should change their behaviours from one place to live in another, even if we graciously ask them to do so. Difficult as it is to impose conditions on immigrants coming into a country to live by their host countries' norms, it is nigh on impossible to impose conditions on their children, short of being willing to punish or expel them.

Other races have their own standards of sorts, perhaps even their own courtesies and etiquette, if only among their own. Many have none towards people of other races, including us. They might be rude by our traditional standards, but not by theirs.

For all our talk of being tolerant, we grew tired of being courteous to people who were not courteous to us. No longer are we the ladies and gentlemen we once were, or aspired to be. The more we became surrounded by rude people, the ruder we became.

Competition, as much as multiculturalism, commanded that we give up our traditional British and other Western niceties. Races frenetic in one country, pushing past each other along their way to whatever they want, do not relax in another, not completely anyway.

We do not realise we have become rude or consider other races rude, because we forget or do not know how polite we used to be. We deride our past civilities, because we deride everything about our past.

The Quest for Multicultural Peace

The overarching objective of our open West is not the pursuit of knowledge, arts, or fulfilment, trying to build the best societies we can. Whether we like racial diversity or meekly accept what we feel powerless to prevent, we deploy an extraordinary amount of time, effort, and resources trying desperately to make multiculturalism work.

Since opening our neighbourhoods and borders to other races, Western governments, educators, and scriptwriters have tried extremely hard to dictate our values and often succeeded. Nevertheless, they have not created commonality across races either based upon diversity or in spite of it. For people to feel morally bound to each other requires a sense of nationalism or other tribalism.

Attempts at multiracial nationalism by white people are only reciprocated by other races when it suits them. It normally only suits them when their numbers are small.

When their numbers are small, minority races must defer to the dominant race and culture. They must behave, according to the norms of that dominant race and culture. They are compelled to conform.

Gathered in groups or alone with the power to act freely, minority races need not behave. The more numerous a race gets, the more it asserts itself, as white people no longer assert ourselves. We do not even defend ourselves or each other.

Immigrant races reap collective benefits from their increasing numbers, growing their political, economic, and cultural clout. The greater their number, the less they defer to us and our culture, the less they need us, and the less likely are we to receive commonality in return.

When we are not trying to change our race, we manage it. We manage white people better than we manage anyone else.

We have to be able to share neighbourhoods with other races, we think, because we have to be able to share the world with them. To question whether different cultures can share a city is to question whether different races can.

It is not an issue outside the West, where countries remain and where races live securely behind borders. Where races do not live separately behind borders, they might live separately within them. Governments and people are not foisting different races together, except to conquer another.

Racial and other homogeneity are natural. Racial diversity is unnatural.

Our white people's burden is to make multiculturalism work, but human nature means that multiculturalism inevitably fails. We think it is our fault that it fails.

It is not. It is racism but not simply racism. Multiculturalism does not recognise how humans actually function.

Teaching Multiculturalism

Before we chanted diversity, the West preached tolerance, until we realised tolerance implied something unpleasant. So, we decided other races do not bring any ills. They bring only good, which we should celebrate.

Our forebears were never as moronic about anything as we are with multiculturalism; we know nothing else. We need to believe certain fundamental tenets about different races living together: that it is necessary, and it is desirable.

Never did the jingoism of our past patriotism rival the jingoism of our postmodern multiculturalism. In education systems where not much is compulsory, events celebrating multiculturalism are compulsory. Teachers lock school gates to prevent students escaping. They patrol surrounding areas in cars.

Like other diversity, we do not debate or really discuss multiculturalism. We celebrate it, mindlessly immersed in idiot slogans.

While our forebears tried improving the world with reason, science, and truth, we imagine creating the world we want with slogans, stickers, and tee shirts. The slogans are beautiful to be sure: love, peace, and unity. The simpler they are, the more we like slogans, but they shut out our chance and our children's chance to learn.

If we did debate, then instead of instilling the children with answers to questions they have not asked, we might pose questions they could ask. If human beings are all the same, how can immigrants enrich us? If cultures are all equal, how can immigrant cultures enrich us?

What successes can multiculturalism boast that racial homogeneity cannot? Why are white people to blame because some races fare poorly, decade after decade, in spite of all the time and money we expend helping them?

Is racial diversity good? Is racism bad? Is multiculturalism worthwhile? Why must we try?

The only points of view we teach our children at school and allow them to utter are those helping other races or maligning ours, in support of multiculturalism. We are telling children what to believe, to the point of pressing them to say it aloud, rather than leaving them to learn from their experiences or the experiences of others. The only imagination we require is finding new ways of saying the same things: how much we like other races around us; how awful things used to be.

If our children do not like multiculturalism, they do not learn public speaking. They do not develop confidence. We do not want people questioning multiculturalism able to address a crowd. We do not want them feeling confident.

Agreeing with our multicultural wonder is easier than thinking or challenging anyone about it. Multiculturalism depends upon it, but being taught endlessly about racial harmony and white people's racism leaves Western schoolchildren less time to learn anything true.

The Death of Truth

We used to say truth was the first casualty of war. It is certainly the first casualty of multiculturalism.

Wherever and whenever different races have lived close together, there has been division and indifference, if not tension and conflict. There is a whole history of racial conflict at white people's expense never mentioned.

In the Haiti genocide of 1804, blacks massacred up to five thousand white men, women, and children to remove white people from the country. Among those massacred were whites who had been friendly to blacks, something we might want to keep in mind. The few exceptions to the massacre included whites willing to marry people of other races: genocide.

Racial and religious tolerance does not require racial and religious integration. It requires a lack of racial and religious integration.

Black violence against white South Africans contributed to

establishing the apartheid regime in that country in 1948. Nevertheless, becoming unable to fathom black violence, we mercilessly condemned white South Africans until apartheid ended in the early 1990s.

With racial homogeneity, there is no problem with racism. Separations across cities become confrontations across neighbourhoods, when different races get close.

Most notably, the racial conflict kept secret was that suffered by white Americans welcoming black Americans into their neighbourhoods through the 1950s and '60s, but then suffering violence and threats of violence because those black Americans had come. We blame racism for white people fleeing those neighbourhoods, without inquiring as to their reasons for leaving.

Western countries draw few lessons from our history about anything. We draw even fewer lessons from the rest of the world. We ignore the past crimes of other races as doggedly as we ignore their crimes today. No amount of violence by other races warrants us associating them with violence.

We only care about the problems of multiculturalism when money is at stake. That is most notably for its impact upon tourism, although we do so without acknowledging race or culture.

Educational Themes

Education is based no longer upon facts, but upon what educators call themes. The most pervasive of those themes are about people.

At best, themes make facts superfluous. We have thematic postmodernism.

At worst, themes can make facts dangerous. Facts might lead people to question the themes we have been taught.

With our devotion to multiculturalism guiding us, we think we open our minds when we believe good things about immigrants. We think we close them when we pay heed to the bad.

Ignorance is not just bliss. We think it is clever.

We only mention other races to applaud them: to laud lovely stories about them. We might praise their supposed bravery for having come, although what was brave about their answering our invitation to come is not obvious. Our colonial forebears who bravely entered hostile environments building countries anew receive no such applause.

Saying good things about other races seems friendly. Any criticism of them or recognition of the challenges we face with them around us becomes boorish.

In support of multiculturalism, we insist that interracial immigration into the West provides only benefits, not costs. The only consequences we contemplate are positive. Anything else, we think would be disrespectful of other races.

Nothing prejudices our perceptions of others. Extolling the wonderful things immigrants supposedly bring to the West means we do not touch upon crime, terror, disease, or social breakdown.

We dismiss the crimes of immigrants because white people commit crimes too, even if the rates of crime by immigrants far exceed those by white people. We treat immigrants knowingly passing on their lethal virus or other communicable disease onto white men and women as no less victims of the virus than those white men or women.

In our hostility to our white racial past, our forebears enjoy no such luxury. We insist that emigration by Europeans to the rest of the world brought only costs, not benefits. The only consequences we contemplate are negative. Maligning the horrors that past European colonialism supposedly brought upon other countries means we talk only about crime, terror, disease, and social breakdown.

We have no regard for the violence committed by indigenous people against each other before we arrived. Nor are we interested in the diseases Europeans suffered.

Not even neutral consequences of either interracial immigration or European colonialism come into our thinking. Europeans coming was an absolute evil, we insist. Everyone else coming is an absolute good, we are certain.

There is, in either case, no rational assessment of the evidence. There is simply a persistent bigotry against white people.

For all our championing diversity, the diversity we applaud when other races come to our countries is one we condemn when we look back to the years white people entered lands that other races occupied. We applaud the changes we claim immigrant races bring to our cultures and landscapes, while applauding indigenous peoples for not changing through centuries, even millennia, before we arrived.

The first arrivals to the Americas, Australasia, and elsewhere supposedly suffered for Europeans coming. The last arrivals supposedly improved our lots. We are the arrivals in between. Colonial Europeans become indebted to immigrants for the good we think they brought us, but remain indebted to indigenous peoples for the ills we think we brought them.

What is never clear through our ideologies of immigration is whether multiracial immigration ameliorates indigenous peoples' suffering across the Americas and Australasia. We simply lump other races together as supposed victims of white people's prejudice, while celebrating them.

The Ideology of Multiculturalism

Societies function in racially and other tribally homogenous countries and regions outside the West. If there is harmony, then racial and religious homogeneity allows it. People do not pretend otherwise.

The ideological West is very different to the rest of the world. It always is.

It is one thing to refuse to consider issues of race and culture when races live apart, as they generally do outside the West. That may simply be institutionalised ignorance.

It is quite another thing to refuse to consider issues of race and culture when other races are allowed, even invited, into our cities, suburbs, and towns. Opening our borders to other races, we should be certain that our compatriots and descendants will not suffer as a result, but we are only certain they will not suffer because of our refusal to consider issues of race and culture. Our certainty is ideological, even emotional, but not intellectual.

We insist that racial diversity and the supposed combination of our racial and religious differences makes multicultural cities and countries strong, without explaining why racial and religious differences should make anywhere strong. We are not so rude as to ask, or even to wonder.

Believing that cultural diversity is our strength makes us happy, when we so much need happiness. We are not so judgemental to adjudicate otherwise, or to examine nations elsewhere.

Instead of rationally examining races and cultures to conclude open borders will not condemn us, we refuse to consider the possibility they might. Instead of identifying the problems of racial diversity so we can try to redress them, we refuse to acknowledge any problems.

When we acknowledge problems, we blame white people. We blame racism, but only white people's racism, without evidence of that racism remaining.

We will abandon our friends with whom we disagree about many an issue, but their race and religion does not affect our opinions of strangers. Unwilling to consider issues of race or culture and unwilling to comprehend the people who do, Western countries have become chock full of people not understanding each other. It is probably better they do not.

There is something extraordinarily evil about an absolute refusal even to consider the possibility that we have growing problems due to interracial immigration. If we cared about our compatriots, we would consider the impact of interracial immigration upon them. If we cared about our descendants, we would recognise that we have more than enough reason to suppose our descendants will suffer more than we suffer from mass immigration.

That evil becomes acute when people deny others the opportunity to consider what they will not consider. We berate people who do consider the possibilities concerning immigration, even without them making any conclusions. We do not imagine that a combination of differences between white people makes *us* strong.

It is one thing to have an idea, such as all cultures being equal or all cultures being compatible. It is one thing to dream of a single world civilisation or simply of multiculturalism in a single country, Europe, or the West.

It is quite another thing to hold steadfast to that dream or idea when people are suffering. That is ideology.

Hubris

Early in the twenty-first century, we judge ourselves for better or worse, try to save the world when it is bad, but know little beyond the walls of our homes. The worlds in which we dream are not other people's worlds.

Few countries outside the West talk of diversity. Those countries that do talk of diversity defend the diversity of people who have been living on their land for centuries. Their diversity is not the result of immigration, as it is in the West.

Their diversity might be the result of national borders being set where they are, as it is in Singapore and Malaysia. Their minority races have lived on the land now part of those countries since before those countries came into being.

Alternatively, their diversity might be the result of conquest after those countries came into being. Countries conquering territory also conquer people already there.

Diversity in Indonesia is the result of both. Its borders upon independence in 1949 were the starting point for the land and people it subsequently conquered.

Those countries do not deny the problems of diversity as we do. They manage them, as best as they can.

The West does not merely promote racial harmony with our newly formed multiculturalism. We insist harmony is already here.

We do not assess interracial immigration and multiculturalism having regard to the totality of the information we have. Instead, we reject talk of race and insist, over and over, that everything is good, or within our power to be good.

American exceptionalism did not begin as an American boast, but as a criticism from communist Soviet dictator Joseph Stalin in 1929. He rejected the view that America was somehow exempt from Marxist theory.

The West thinks we are exceptional, able to create multiracial societies nobody else has. All around the West there are countries boasting that they are the most successful multicultural countries on earth. We do so by acknowledging some of the problems of multiculturalism in other countries, but blocking from our minds the problems in our own.

Even the most rudimentary questioning of our supposed success with multiculturalism would be racist. We refuse to be racist.

The few countries outside the West with multiculturalism might highlight it in their tourism advertisements for a West that thinks nothing is more wonderful than multiculturalism, but that is about all. They do not pretend to be the most successful multicultural countries on earth, whatever that means.

We persist with interracial immigration in spite of its appalling record, certain we are succeeding with multiculturalism, without explaining what constitutes success. Multiculturalism succeeds, because we say it succeeds.

No amount of destruction or violence when multiculturalism goes wrong keeps us from feeling enlightened: that ours is the most successful multicultural country on earth. A hundred immigrants could storm our streets beheading a thousand people of our race, but we would still declare multiculturalism a success, while white people elsewhere change the colours on their computer pages in sympathy for the victims.

The Failure of Multiracial Liberalism

"Free institutions are next to impossible in a country made up of different nationalities," wrote liberal philosopher John Stuart Mill in 1859. *"Among people without fellow-feeling, especially if they read and speak different languages, the united public opinion, necessary to the working of representative government, cannot exist."*

Fellow feeling is nationalism, racism, or other tribalism. That lack of fellow feeling also makes freedom of speech, democracy, universal suffrage, an independent judiciary, and other cornerstones of classic liberalism incompatible with multiracialism. It is the same lack of fellow feeling with Western individualism, but at least we find a common opinion to demand individualism.

The West averted the problem of a lack of a united public opinion by governing with little recourse to public opinion. We dismiss public opinion for being populism.

Integrating immigrants is multiracialism without multiculturalism. Multiculturalism expects immigrants not to integrate. Both are unworkable in free democracies.

The rights and liberties that functioned among white communities are not functioning among other races. With the coming of individualism and end of white communities, they are not functioning much better among white people anymore.

Multiculturalism is not liberalism. Liberalism has proven incompatible with interracial immigration, as we never imagined when we opened our borders and as we still refuse to confront.

Before 1945, any thoughtful person asked to foreshadow the

consequences of mass immigration and racial integration would have spoken of problems among those that have arisen, without contemplating our determination to try so hard and our willingness to give up so much in pursuit of our multicultural ideal. It took two world wars and a holocaust to make us try.

The Failure of Multicultural Liberalism

Our multicultural vision presumes justice is objective. It is not. Without connectedness, one person's justice is often injustice to a person from another race or religion. Justice is subjective.

Expecting people from other races and religions to accept Western laws, including criminal laws, they have not drafted is racist and religiously discriminatory. Some of them point that out, when they assert their alternatives. We tacitly admit so, when we accommodate their alternatives.

Without comparing cultures or belittling any religion, the only religions aside from Christianity that Western liberalism can accommodate are those that adherents keep close to their communities, like Judaism, and those that are not important. Islam is important. Its adherents do not confine their religion to their communities.

Free speech was a cornerstone of liberalism. It has proven incompatible with multiculturalism.

We control what we say, but we have to do that. We fear the repercussions otherwise.

In spite of our best efforts, Muslims in the West constantly fear being insulted as they do not fear in Muslim countries. When we err by what might seem to us a trivial degree, their pride, faith, and collective identities (unimaginable to us) compel them to react, violently if need be.

Muslims own their holidays. We do not even own ours. If we are not striving hard to overcome the complications of accommodating Islamic culture, we are denying those complications.

Intrinsic to multiculturalism are tensions that racial and religious homogeneity do not suffer. Multicultural environments are innately more prone to violence, because the energy for which we enthuse becomes conflict whenever someone feels aggrieved.

Without respect for race, religion, and other human interests, liberalism becomes another ideology stampeding over people. It is no less confrontational and provocative than any other ideology.

With respect for other races and their religions but without willingness to assert our own, liberalism meekly surrenders to those other races and their religions. Liberalism dissolves.

Either way, multiculturalism requires increasing authoritarianism, even totalitarianism: the end of liberalism. Racial and religious diversity requires increased surveillance and other security: a role for the state tantamount to social dictatorship. A world without borders is a world of conflict and turmoil, until martial law takes control.

Commercial Relationships

Western cities went through the Great Depression, wartime and post-war austerity, and other crises with little if any violence. With nationalism, we had senses of society, quite apart from whether we had jobs or whether shops were open to trade.

It took the four-year Social War for her to do so, but Rome granted citizenship to fellow Italians in 87 B.C. She did not see Sicilians, Sardinians, or Corsicans as fellow Italians.

A rare instant of a nation voluntarily granting citizenship to other races before the Second World War was the *Constitutio Antoniniana* of 212 A.D. Emperor Caracalla extended Roman citizenship to all free men of the Roman Empire and offered all women the rights of Roman women, with some exceptions.

Caracalla's motivations remain unclear, but it was a grant of legal rights and privileges. Rome seems not to have imagined societies encompassing more than one race. With the Empire already in decline, the *Constitutio Antoniniana* did not help.

Taking servants of some form or another was the only basis upon which any society welcomed other races into their countries in any material numbers, until the West did after World War II. They remain a major plank of Western immigration programmes. We call them employees.

Societies always collapse after taking other races for their servants. We think we create community with jobs, giving people a stake in economic society, but it is not enough.

As much with multiculturalism as with individualism, the West has become fixated with economics because we have to be. We are trying to give people economic reasons to co-operate with each other, when they have no other reasons.

Without the unifying influence of a common race or religion, people need monetary reasons to co-operate with each other, to maintain civic order. The only interests individuals and races have in each other are commercial. The primary relationships between individuals and between races are earning money and spending it.

We are no longer countries. We are economies.

We are no longer communities. We are commercial transactions.

We believe race has vanished from our cities because we see different races operating stores adjoining each other, even shopping in each other's stores, without any sense of anything but commercial enterprise. Racial harmony means storekeepers not fighting each other. Shoplifting is presumably fine.

Shopping is our parameter. We define people by their purchases, instead of their race.

Western countries are no longer functioning societies in any meaningful way, beyond economic transactions, not as they used to function. Economic transactions are not society. Two or more transactions to which people are party are simply business relationships.

The only racial or religious integration is pecuniary. Some people do not even have that.

Generosity without Gratitude

With no history of empire or African slavery, racially homogenous Sweden believed she would overcome the problems of multiculturalism in other countries by giving immigrants citizenship and generous government welfare benefits so they had no need to work or pay taxes, while undertaking a plethora of programmes promoting racial integration. Sweden was wrong.

Welcoming immigrants does not make them like us or be like us. Generosity does not make recipients into the people that donors want them to be, or presume they already are.

Immigrants had not worked to come and not worked for the

money Sweden gave them on arrival. Without nationalism or other fellow feeling joining benefactors and beneficiaries, sharing a country's wealth and resources creates a sense of entitlement among the beneficiaries. Subsequently expecting immigrants to start working for their next government benefit becomes unfair.

The problems of interracial immigration do not become less with generations born in their new lands. They become worse. Even if some refugees and other immigrants happen to feel at least a little obligation and gratitude to their Western hosts for welcoming them, their children and grandchildren feel no obligations.

They do not even feel gratitude. Indeed, they expressly reject the suggestion they should feel grateful to Western countries and people who admitted them and give them so much.

The generosities we grant mean nothing. They have no reason to appreciate the refuge, home, and money we grant them because we tell them they have rights to whatever we give them. The more we encourage them to think we are obliged to help them, the more they demand.

We do not just indulge immigrants their ingratitude. We reward it. We keep giving them more, imagining there might come a time when they feel we have given them enough, when they might even like us.

There will not come such a time. They have no cause to value what we give them, but every cause to demand more. The more we help other races, the greater their expectations become.

We think thugs become angels when we welcome them to our countries, giving them houses and healthcare. However often people from other races harm or kill people of our race, we will still put our arms around them and give more. Being nice to warlords, telling them how lovely they are, we are sure they will soon come around.

Other races do not help as we help. They are thus not constantly criticised for not doing more to help, as we are criticised.

The West giving other races so much only makes them crosser for what we have not given them. Not getting everything they want makes them angry.

Expending enough money and with enough education, we think money can buy anything and schools can teach anything, including multicultural harmony, but our battle against race is a battle against reality. It is an unwinnable battle we keep waging.

If the West is trying to demonstrate to the world that people are all individuals and that countries are superfluous, then more than half a century after we began racial integration, all we have shown is that people are tribal and boundaries between tribes are necessary. If we are trying to prove that different races can live together freely and harmoniously, then we are only proving they cannot, not even with our wealth and welfare payments.

Money does not engage people. It simply funds them. Trying to hold multiracial landscapes together requires huge sums of money, but no amount of money changes human or racial natures.

Expectations of Equality

Among our problems is that we no longer recognise that people are different, that races are different. They are different.

Hearing us declare that everyone is equal and that all races are equal, we have created expectations of equality, even among people who do not study or work as hard as we study and work, or are less skilled and intelligent than we are. They complain their lives are not as good as are ours.

We encourage people of other races to expect everything their Western hosts enjoy, and not simply the poorest or average among their hosts and hostesses. They see the lifestyles of the richest white people and expect equality with them.

Immigration means racial conflicts become class conflicts too, while traditional class conflicts become lost among racial conflicts. Class conflicts become racial conflicts.

Without race to blame, immigrants blame white people's racism for their not enjoying the lives of the richest white people. White people keep aiding other races, but still most immigrants remain not as rich as the richest of us, or even the average among us. There is a sense of hopelessness.

People seeing others fare better than they fare feel frustrated. The more they fall short of what we assure them they deserve, to live as we live, the more virulent their frustrations.

Immigrants who could have been peaceful in their countries become violent in ours. People who were violent in their countries remain violent in ours.

Even if we redistribute all our wealth to make races equal, people are not equal. A person in a racially homogenous country or from a dominant race in a racially diverse environment not getting a job, prize, or anything else is more likely to hold himself or herself responsible. A person from a racial minority is less likely to do so.

No matter how many successful people hail from a minority race, people from that race failing to get something they want will blame prejudice from any race they feel is more powerful than theirs. Feeling they have been unfairly denied their success, they are uninterested in the successes of other people of their race and in the failures of people from that relatively more powerful race.

Racial diversity leads people to blame other races for their failings and misadventure. Racial homogeneity means people are more likely to take responsibility for their lives and actions.

Unwilling to take action against any race but our own and certain that white people's prejudice pressures everyone else, the only solution we imagine is winding back white dominance, but the problems will remain. There will still be failings and misadventure, but we can all feel frustrated. If we ever recognise that races other than ours can be prejudiced too, we can all blame prejudice for whatever we lack that someone from another race has and for whatever we miss out upon that someone from another race gets.

Rioting and Crime

Multiculturalism fails when the economic incentives for civic order run out. Eventually they do, periodically in free market economies.

While looters and rioters of other races unashamedly post their faces onto social media, Western news media prefer to publish pictures of white rioters, if there are any. We seize upon white rioters to dissociate rioting from race, no matter how few they are and how many people of other races run amok.

A single white culprit is reason to dismiss consideration of race, although we dissociate race from rioting and crime even without any white culprits. Any number of rich rioters is not a reason for us to dismiss consideration of class.

Obsessed as we are with economics, economic factors remain our favourite fingers of blame for rioting and crime, although they caused less rioting and crime before other races came. Fixated as we have become about money, we assume other races are too.

Unemployment and limited employment opportunities are a focus, although they still seem to inspire less crime among white people than among other races. Jobs are supposed to occupy people's minds, distracting them from criminal endeavours, as if that is all people with free minds want to do. The onus of avoiding more violence by finding employment for people of other races is upon white people, because the onus to do everything is upon white people.

Among our favourite excuses for crime by other races is a lack of government support. Averting their crimes is thus neither our responsibility nor theirs. It is the government's responsibility.

Thus, we do not punish other races for crimes their people commit. Instead, our governments and we give them more money or spend even more money upon them, hoping the next tranche we give them or spend upon them will avert them from committing crime, although every previous tranche has not.

Money is supposed to prevent crime because it lets people buy things to consume what remains of their time. Without work and consumerism, there is only reality.

Rather than blame thieves and looters for rioting and other crime, we blame ourselves. We blame consumer advertising for inspiring thieves and looters to want more, although that too seems to inspire less crime among white people than among other races.

We who understand only economies being important reduce rich people's crimes to greed and poor people's crimes to poverty, but greed is unending and poverty relative. A rich African in Africa might have less wealth than a poor African in America.

Racial conflicts arise when people feel they suffer economically. Amidst racial diversity, some people feel they suffer because they see people nearby faring better.

We arbitrarily define poverty in terms of a percentage of the population overall: the poorest ten percent or whatever. Whatever our definitions, there will always be poor.

Finding poor people jobs or otherwise increasing their wealth consequently categorises other people as poor, perhaps from that same race. Statistics barely change.

To avoid economic inequality and thus resentment, multiculturalism requires economic totalitarianism: communism.

Then we can be equally poor.

The End of Authority

Without the threat of punishment, the only effective authorities are within families and other tribes. In much of the world, tribespeople do not defer to authorities outside their tribes, not even others of their race. There are still crimes within communities, but people peaceful within their communities become violent in other environments.

We would rarely have accepted instructions from other races before World War II. Our increasing enthusiasm for doing so since then has made other races less willing than ever to take instructions from us.

People of other races heed the leaders of their race, not other races, as regards anything important. Only white people invite people of other races to tell us what to do.

Among the costs of interracial immigration we never consider, multiracial workforces are more difficult to manage than racially homogenous workforces. People of other races might take instructions from their own, provided they do not see their own as our instruments.

Western individualism and multiculturalism are never more obviously intertwined than in the end of any sense of authority, structure, or society. Social structures arise with the force not of law but nationalism, racism, and other tribalism, which we have dismissed. Like people from other races, we individuals only respect Western authority when doing so is in our individual interests.

Authorities might be sporting umpires or anyone else. When the West comprised societies, school teachers reprimanding students could expect support from the students' parents. Without such authority, many parents add to a problem.

At some schools, teachers and others have been found more likely to reprimand certain races for disruption, violence, and other unruly behaviour. In our rejection of race and racism, we do not reprimand unruly children. We reprimand schools and teachers for reprimanding unruly children.

Unable to consider that other races could really be more unruly than ours, when confronted with disproportionate misbehaviour by other races, we blame racial discrimination. In the ethos of multiculturalism, we link wrongdoing not to the wrongdoers' race but to white people's racism, even where there are no white people around.

The impact of those children's unruly behaviour upon the education of other children is immaterial, because education has become relatively immaterial to the West. Tolerance and diversity matter more.

In the name of fairness and equity, we ceased being concerned with discipline. Instead, we seek conflict resolution, with a smile. We imagine making everything fine with a hug.

We forgive or ignore misbehaviour previously unacceptable among white children and adults. To avoid restricting other races, we might relax our rules for everyone, including white children and adults. We might just relax our rules for other races.

The rules of multiculturalism demand respect for other races, not ours. White people are not interested in keeping face ourselves, but we submit to Asians wanting to keep face.

Other races also expect respect from us, without giving what they do not have to give. They respect their own.

The End of Policing

Whether we recognise that people of other races only respect authority from people within their race or it is another expression of our endless devotion to diversity, our police forces particularly like hiring officers from other races. As we implicitly acknowledge, race does not vanish when a person puts on a uniform. Police officers of other races are still people of their race.

When those police enforce Western laws, people of their race see them as collaborators with us: traitors. Conversely, those police might simply not enforce our laws. We often do not.

Our traditionally relaxed British policing fails to police people of other races. When people of other races alert the police to prospective crimes, it is to protect their own from harm, either from other criminals or from the police response. They do not report criminals of their race to the police *after* those criminals committed their crimes.

The only culture we blame for crime is our own. So does everyone else.

Immigrants say we are culpable for the crimes they commit because Western cultures include a flurry of freedoms in which we bask, but which free other races to be criminal. Immigrants come from countries where criminals can be caned, gaoled, and executed into a West where they are given healthcare, legal services, food, clothing, and counselling. Criminals enjoy more rights in the West than law-abiding citizens enjoy elsewhere.

The feelings of community that once connected us with our police no longer connect us. Other races' feelings of community have never connected them with our police. Policing only adds to our problems.

Inevitably, people of any race but ours do not trust police of another race. They often do not trust police of their own race in Western countries, for seeing them as instruments of governments and countries not their own. They want police to leave them alone, but foisted in close proximity to each other, multiculturalism means we cannot leave each other alone, not all the time.

Rather than give up on multiculturalism, we give up on policing. Like the rest of us, our police try desperately to connect with other races. Our police pose, dance, and march with people of other races no matter how criminal those other races are, hoping that will make other races like them.

Immigrants thus blame their crime upon Western governments and police for being too lax with criminals. They do not blame their crime upon Western governments for allowing interracial immigration.

Neither do we, because we do not see the link between immigration and crime. We are more likely to blame Western governments for not doing even more to submit to other races. We blame Western police for policing, instead of dancing more often.

It becomes reasonable to suppose that countries outside the West are autocratic because they need to be autocratic to control their people. That is quite apart from trying to control anyone else.

In addition to their government authorities, other countries have tribal and religious authorities, supplementing or defying those government authorities. Those other authorities defying the government authorities command the government authorities to be still more authoritarian.

Not just relaxed British and other Western policing fail with other races. So do relaxed British and other Western parenting.

If we are open to the possibility of there being differences between races, then those differences might be psychological. Given their natures, other races might not be suited to liberalism, let alone our gentle British Bobbies.

The West did not need to be autocratic with only our own and small numbers of other races and particular other races to govern, before so many immigrants from other races came. Governing some races (wherever they happen to be) requires more laws and policing than we spent governing our racially homogenous selves.

If we are not going to free the aggression of other races to harm us and each other, we must live without liberties we take for granted. Multiculturalism requires social totalitarianism, such as communism.

The Relevance and Irrelevance of Race

Western political and community leadership demands keeping racism dormant, if only among white people. Trying to curtail the conflicts and frictions of racial diversity, police and media withhold information.

In our culturally sensitive treatment of crime, criminals are merely known to police. Those assaulting police are simply unco-operative.

People living near large numbers of immigrants are much less welcoming of immigrants than people living near fewer immigrants. The less we encounter other races, the more we like them.

Media campaigns mould our minds, but paradoxically, campaigns promoting tolerance of immigrants exacerbate racism. That might be because they confront people accustomed not to thinking of other races.

Multiculturalism is a failed ideology, but we refuse to let go of our multiracial ideals. Doggedly we hang onto the dream. Letting go of our globalist ideals can be as hard as other races but ours would find letting go of their countries.

Believing only what we say are the benefits of multiculturalism, we would rather wallow in a broken hovel than think we are wrong about diversity being such a strength or about immigrants enriching our lives, culturally or otherwise. We would rather wallow than admit we are just ordinary, no better able to create multicultural societies than any other people have been through history or any other people are in the world today.

We have made race and religion relevant whenever mentioning them promotes racial or religious diversity. We have made race and religion irrelevant whenever mentioning them does not promote racial or religious diversity.

Thus, we fail to see the badness in other races, however prevalent that badness might be. We see only the good in other races and in racial diversity, however rare that goodness might be.

With the rules of racism and religion we impose, multiculturalism cannot help but seem to succeed. We come to think well of people we have never met.

Other races generally care less what we think of them than we care. So desperate are we to defend our multicultural dream, we are far more determined that other races look good than they are, even their community leaders and other spokespeople playing politics are. They have no need to be good when we insist they are good, whatever they do.

We do not simply fear the social disharmony that might result from public knowledge of the race and religion of criminals. We fear the increased opposition to interracial immigration and multiculturalism that might ensue.

Just as importantly, the truth would be offensive, to white people certain that we have created multicultural communities. Suggesting everything is not peachy among a multitude of races would be a gruesome, bleak thing to do.

Linking race and reality can seem churlish and nasty to people happily unaware, inviting them to consider matters too horrible to contemplate. We prefer nicety to reality.

Crime and Racism

Unable to imagine criminals being more likely to be of one race than another, and often unable to imagine people of other races being criminals at all, we do not imagine crime causing racial tensions. Instead, we imagine police or media mentioning a criminal's or suspected criminal's race causing racial tensions.

We blame crime not upon race but upon racism, our racism, especially police racism, in spite of every effort the police make to appease other races and to keep their crimes secret. Police–community relations depend upon police tolerating crimes by other races we would not tolerate by our own.

When police do not tolerate crimes, police pleas for public help in finding suspects can require police to mention the most obvious descriptors of suspects' physical appearances. We like white criminals. It means criminal diversity.

Suspected criminals of other races are ideologically problematic. Where we can rely upon something other than race to describe them, we do.

With their lack of trust in police, identifying criminal suspects by a minority race makes people of that minority race feel distrusted. The more common the crime among people of their race, the more likely they are to hear their race described as the race of a suspect, and the more they feel police are prejudiced against them. We thus bar police from using racial descriptors.

Another reason we bar police from using racial descriptors is to prevent public prejudice concerning which races are most responsible for crime. That we feel the need to bar racial descriptions suggests that any such prejudice is well founded.

While police are still seeking suspects in a crime, racial traits and even racial appearance might get a mention because we have lost our sense that there are racial traits or racial appearances. Even then, those racial traits and appearances are only mentioned to a local audience able to help. National and international news services are even less likely than local news services to reveal the race of a suspect.

Without white pangs about racism, criminals can taunt, assault, and even kill white people for being white. We still will not mention those criminals' race.

More often than not, we water racial descriptions down to skin tones. Criminal suspects can have brown or dark skin, much like white people who sit too long in the sun.

Policing does not come into it. Refusing to reveal the race of a criminal suspect hampers police in their job, possibly preventing suspects being caught, but police are willing to let suspects evade arrest rather than revealing their race to others.

Feelings matter. Prejudice matters. Crime matters less.

Understanding between cultures depends upon police and media concealing the facts about crime from a populace that would rather be ignorant and wrong than lose confidence in multiculturalism. In the clash between racial harmony and catching criminals, even preventing further crime or saving the country, we want harmony. Faux harmony is better than none.

Crime and Race

An argument opposing the identification of the races of criminal suspects is that the identification is only a guess, but it can be a pretty good guess. To anyone not determined to shut down consideration of race, identifying a person's race is normally obvious.

When police have the name of a suspect, with all the records of that suspect at hand, identifying his or her race might be even more obvious. When the suspect is in custody or court, his or her race should be inescapable, even if it is a mishmash of races.

Yet, whatever might be reported when police are searching for suspected criminals, all mention of their racial traits disappears when police apprehend them. Identifying a suspect allows for all manner of information about the person to become known, but their race and religion remain secrets.

At one level, we do not contemplate that some races could be more criminal than others because crime is not exclusive to any. There could be a thousand times more wrongdoers from another race than ours, but all we need to dispel any link between race and crime is one criminal who is not of that race.

At another level, everyone from another race being bad would not sway us. We still would not notice. We reject any link between race and crime (unless the race is Western and the crime is our past imperialism, racism, and so forth) because we reject racism. It is an ideological rejection, not an intellectual rejection.

For all our efforts to remove reporting the races of criminals, a world of inference has developed among people willing to think about things. It is a netherworld that deduces that certain races are more likely than other races to commit particular crimes, among all manner of matters we never say loudly.

Adding to our difficulties is how little we know. In Britain, the Home Office refuses to compile statistics of the races or religions of criminals. For all our decades of multiculturalism, we have no data at all.

In 1996, the Swedish National Council for Crime Prevention reported North African immigrants to be twenty-three times more likely to commit rape than Swedish men. Sweden did not cease interracial immigration. She ceased racial statistics.

France banned the creation of racial files altogether, quite apart from matters of crime. Whatever relationship race might have with anything, there is not to be one.

Yet even impartial computer algorithms link certain races to crime, while conducting no racial profiling. With their businesses and money depending upon reality, bail companies and other advertisers link some races to crime but not others.

Crime and Indulgence

Averting crime is no reason for us to talk about race. Indulging criminals is.

Our criminal justice systems convict and gaol particular races in proportions much higher than their proportions of the general populations, even the young or poor populations, warrant. Certain as we are that all races are equal, or that races are not real, we are consequently certain that no race could be more criminal than any other. Therefore, we conclude our criminal justice systems must be racist. Other races' crimes become our disgrace, not theirs.

When we recognise the races of criminals from races other than ours, especially those races already over-represented in the criminal justice system, it is to excuse them, in all or in part. Justice can see after all.

Rather than risk racial disharmony, we let criminals from other races go free or incur lesser punishments, perhaps to commit crimes again. Doing so mitigates the statistics we keep secret or do not compile anyway.

When Western countries and jurisdictions, especially colonial European countries, record the race of criminals among their statistics, it is to find means of being culturally sensitive towards criminals of other races. That is to say, it is to alter our criminal justice system to excuse them.

They might enjoy laxer standards or additional procedures before being punished. We might simply leave them alone.

Crime is inevitable amidst multiculturalism. It is also defensible.

Race remains relevant to crime whenever people of another race plead it in their defence. Rather than refusing to recognise race, we often let a wrongdoer's race mitigate culpability.

Put another way, some races being more criminal than others for whatever reason or reasons, our determined desire for racial equality demands we treat races unequally. Our ideologies of equality require racism to other races' benefit. Absurd it might be, but our rejection of racism requires racism.

Responsibility for rehabilitating criminals is not theirs. It is ours.

We support them, with sympathy, counselling, and money. Everything wrong with other races being white people's fault can be tiresome.

Immigrant Privilege

When immigrants engage in otherwise unpalatable actions or idleness and even when they wrong us, we indulge them by saying they are not used to our ways. Cultural differences are often our justification to excuse other races, however many years, decades, or generations they have lived in the West.

The cultural differences we are supposed to celebrate can be difficult for them, we acknowledge, as we do not acknowledge those cultural differences being difficult for white people. Their crimes against white people become merely cultural misunderstandings.

When their children wrong us, we blame our schools and society. Without notions of race to distinguish them from our sons and daughters, we blame all of us together.

They do not make those excuses. We do.

When indigenous people wrong colonial Europeans, there is European colonisation to blame. White people are not free to blame our crimes and other wrongdoing upon immigration by other races as indigenous people are free to blame their crimes and other wrongdoing upon European colonisation.

Indulging other races is not racist, we insist. It is racial sensitivity.

We are most forgiving of crime and other wrongdoing by other races when white people are victims. When people from other races attack us, we refuse to be racist. We forgive the wrongdoers.

There is no white privilege. There is an immigrant privilege and in colonial European countries an indigenous privilege, which denies, ignores, and excuses other races their crimes and misbehaviours. Rights and entitlements have become inalienable, whatever people's behaviour, as is our confidence in other races.

A risk of prejudice could be a reason for races to behave. Were we to let misbehaviour, crime, and terror by other races give rise to prejudice against them, there might be reason for their community leaders to try to curtail crime among their own to improve their reputation.

Instead of reducing the risk of crime, we reduce the risk of prejudice. The misbehaviour, crime, and terror remain.

It might even worsen. Other races know that nothing bad they do can diminish the esteem in which white people hold them. The more they wrong us, the more we indulge them.

Nothing they do can have consequences. Why would they not continue to harm us?

Biological Bases of Criminality

The problems of multiculturalism are not simply people being bad. Physical differences between races discourage sensible people from playing sports where people of other races trample on them.

There are also psychological differences between races. Some races are quicker to anger than others.

The Polynesian instinct is not to talk through feelings. Polynesians express their emotion physically, including through violence.

By favouring some genes over others, evolution might influence human behaviour. Environments where violent people are more likely to survive and procreate would tend to make populations of people living there more violent. Tribes, ethnic groups, and races could become increasingly violent over generations. Violence begets violence.

Human instinct might not be to harm people without reason.

Some races are quick to find reason.

Before World War II, scientists investigated possible biological bases for criminal behaviour and other social problems. The Jewish Holocaust ended those inquiries.

Nazi eugenics still frightens the West from considering biological bases for human behaviour even where there is no correlation with race, unless the race is ours. Our fears of another Holocaust shut down an entire field of science: of inquiry.

Some loosely related fields of science, much smaller in their scope, endure, to a point. The science of epigenetics examines environmental impacts upon human brains, regulating the expression of innate genetic codes. Recognising any role for genes in human behaviour opens up the theoretical possibility that biology can make some people more likely to be violent and criminal.

There might be genes for anything: warfare, psychiatric illness, alcoholism, obesity, and so forth. In most cases, people control their behaviour, overriding their behavioural genetics, if they wish. Many people do not control their behaviour, especially in environments where they have no incentive to control it. Many areas within the West have become such environments, at least for other races.

In 1994, British neuroscientist Adrian Raine reported evidence that a combination of birth complications and early maternal rejection of babies had significant correlation with individuals becoming violent criminals as adults. Critics denounced his work as racist, although there was no obvious relation to race.

In 2011, neuroscientist David Eagleman believed that brain tumours could cause criminal behaviour. Eagleman was Jewish.

By 2013, Raine's work linked genetics and brains with criminality. He acknowledged that environmental factors might play a role.

In 2014, Finnish physician Jari Tiihonen attributed around five to ten percent of violent crime in Finland to a monoamine oxidase A genotype and the CDH13 gene. He linked that genotype and gene to at least ten homicides, attempted homicides, and batteries.

The environment remains important. Factors such as suffering abuse early in life can massively increase the likelihood of criminal behaviour. Without those factors, genes alone might have little influence.

Scarred by the Holocaust, the West continues to reject any biological basis for criminality. We have become confident that education can overcome race and other biology, in spite of the evidence otherwise. Many future despots from outside the West enjoyed Western tutelage in their youth, before growing up to threaten the West. We nevertheless remain confident that people born in the West become like us even if their immigrant parents are not, although nine hundred years in Europe have not made the Roma less gypsy.

Ideologically Acceptable Aspects of Crime

With any unlawful or socially undesirable action, there are two distinct lines of inquiry and response. The first focuses upon the individual perpetrator and any accomplices directly or indirectly involved. The second looks to broader factors that might have contributed to those perpetrators and accomplices acting as they did.

Certain that different races can live together, we look for something other than race or racial diversity to blame for rioting and crime. The only causes of crime we contemplate are environmental, but not multiculturalism. We have disallowed race and racial diversity as reasons for anything bad.

Nor do we think too much about family breakdown, except in economic terms. Family breakdown contributes to men becoming criminals, but the West refuses to contemplate reasons to keep families together any more than we contemplate reasons to keep races together. They are both too biological.

Among environmental causes of crime, we consider all sorts of political, social, and economic forces, but not other races nearby. Those forces we consider include the treatment of women and children along with social isolation, although not in the context of race or religion.

We blame poor schools for crime, although teachers are too busy with diversity to do very much else. We blame bad parenting, the law, and society, which we also expect to create in people a stake in society that diverse environments lack.

Preoccupied as we are with economic and material indices, we might link any other force with economic considerations. They underpin the characteristics we consider most relevant in the descriptions of criminals and suspected criminals.

A person's income or poverty is always relevant to our deliberations about crime and thus our descriptions of criminals. Being homeless is a particularly useful descriptor. Receiving government welfare payments would be relevant, much as a job would be, for its financial implications, without wondering whether it correlates with race.

Even a statistic correlating with race we dismiss. We might dismiss it for the numbers being too small. We might simply dismiss it.

Criminal Descriptions

Certain there are no links between race or religion and the risk of bad behaviour, what remains is an abundance of other features we consider relevant to describing criminals and criminal suspects. We freely mention their gender, age, height, weight, or build, as well as their clothes, hairstyle, facial hair, teeth, and even their overbite, when we know of it.

Hair is a particular favourite among our post-racial descriptors. Hair colour can be ideal, especially when it is unnatural. A streak of dye will suffice.

The clothes criminals wear while committing crimes or in court can make reports more interesting to read. So too can descriptions of small scars on their cheeks.

In reporting the characteristics of criminals and criminal suspects, race is not relevant, but relatives are. Being a parent is relevant to our descriptions of criminals, as being a child of divorced parents is not.

Even bicycles are relevant. That might be because we do not mind generalisations about cyclists. It might be because we want bicycles mentioned.

Music is relevant, if it is country or western music. We can only imagine white people, and poor rural white people at that, listening to country or western music. Nobody minds people's prejudices against white people, especially poor rural white people.

Strangely enough, words of detail include residency and nationality of any Western country, knowing it can be of any race, even if the criminals and their friends never describe themselves as such. Identifying criminals' residency or nationality can be more problematic for countries outside the West, where nationality and residency connote a race. We can still get it wrong.

Being an immigrant is only relevant to our descriptions of criminals who have immigrated from other Western countries. We describe them as immigrants unabashed, making it clear the Western countries from which they came. People presume they are white.

There is a game around the races of criminals, for anyone willing to play. More fun than reading reports is deciphering them.

Some criminals' names suggest their race. Other names reveal little.

From mention of some suburbs or cities of residence, we can infer a criminal's race. A criminal's job being a liaison officer, even a police liaison officer, with a particular race or races, is telling.

Investigators interviewing a suspect might require the aid of a particular interpreter. It makes the suspect sound like a victim, estranged from us.

Race is irrelevant to our descriptions of criminals. Language is not.

The legal representation of an alleged criminal might also reveal much about the criminal. The Aboriginal Legal Service gets a lot of work defending clients accused of burglary and assault, but not so much of corporate fraud or embezzlement.

Tolerance of Crime and Terror

Countries outside the West do not need unpleasant, awful, or even fatal consequences of immigration to refuse immigration. Protecting its people from crime and terror has nevertheless been cited as a reason that aging Japan does not allow other races to settle there, notwithstanding the crimes and occasionally even terror that Japanese commit against each other. We respect other races' rationales for refusing immigration we would not allow ourselves, because we respect other races.

Fundamentally, the West tolerates crime and terror. We forgive. We forget. We ignore.

We were not so tolerant of criminals and terrorists before

World War II. We have many reasons for indulging them now.

In spite of so much morality being remarkably uniform across races and cultures, morality is intrinsically cultural. Losing confidence in our cultures, we lost confidence in our moralities.

Our cultural relativism becomes moral relativism, making one people's morality no better than another people's morality. Moral relativism (that is to say, amorality) leaves us without grounds upon which to judge people good or evil.

Multiculturalism means we are unwilling to impose our cultures upon other races. We are this unwilling to impose moral values upon other races.

Individualism means we are unwilling to impose moral values upon our race. Underlying morality is empathy, but we are too individualistic to empathise with victims of crime and terror.

We are satisfied simply not to be victims ourselves: that riots are not erupting in the streets outside our homes, breaking our bedroom windows. Being only individuals, we have no sense of being societies, races, or nations to defend from crime or anything else.

In the conflict between individual and collective interests, we hold steadfast to individuals, no matter how awful those individuals are. The rest of the world favours societies. We could do the same by perceiving victim societies made up of victim individuals, but we do not so perceive.

Through it all, and without us admitting it, we cosset criminals because proportionately so many more of them are from races other than ours. In our determination to be kind, racial tolerance demands we tolerate crime.

We blame circumstance for crime. We blame ourselves. We do not blame race or racial diversity.

We accept crime as bad luck or a turn of fate and it is: multicultural bad luck and fate. We become blasé.

While we do not impose morality upon others, we impose ideology upon each other in this Age of Ideology. Multiculturalism is an ideology. It requires an ideology of tolerance of other races, however criminal they are. We only fret about racism.

Freedom of movement is one for criminals as much as for everyone else. If immigrants remained in their countries of origin, then they might attack someone there. Without racism or nationalism, the West has no problem with Western victims taking the places of victims from other races in other countries. We might even prefer it, in the name of equality.

Refugees raping white women and children are not a reason for the West to refuse those refugees asylum. Nothing can be serious enough for that. It is a reason for compassion, although not for the women and children.

Victims of Colour

Crimes by people of other races against white people involve no social issues we want to explore. Indeed, quite the opposite. The last thing we want to do is promote white people's prejudice.

We generalise not the criminals of other races, but the victims. For the race, religion, or refugee status of other races involved in crime or other wrongdoing to be relevant to our descriptions and consideration of them, they should be not the criminal but the victim.

Britain's refusal to compile statistics of the race or religion of criminals does not deter the Home Office from publishing statistics of the race or religion of victims: of hate crimes against Jews and Muslims. We worry not about crime and terror *by* Muslims, but about rudeness *towards* them.

While we refuse to consider such a concept as Muslim crime or terror, we are certain of Muslim victimhood. Since the Holocaust, we have become certain of every race and religion's victimhood, except ours.

We tolerate the crimes of other races, unless their victims are also not white. Never are we more concerned for the victims of crime and terror than we are when they are of races other than ours. We do not blame them for being lax, provocative, or insensitive as we often blame white victims of crime. We dwell upon those victims as we do not dwell upon white victims.

So when someone of another race commits a crime against someone else of another race, the race of that poor victim is relevant but the race of the perpetrator is not, even when they are of the same race. Only if we can cast the perpetrator as a victim too, especially of our supposed white racism, will his race come to the fore.

White Criminals

For the race of a criminal to be relevant to his description in a news report, simple conversation, or thoughts in our head, the criminal must be white. If the criminal is not white, we make him white.

A white Hispanic is a Hispanic who killed, even in self-defence. Good Hispanics remain simply Hispanic.

Few things assure us more of our rejection of racism than white criminals. They convince us there would still be crime if our countries had remained racially homogeneous. We then end the thought process, without contemplating the impact that interracial immigration has on white people: the social breakdown, the economic cost, the hopelessness and despair becoming essentially stateless. We do not pose the question whether there might be less crime by white people without other races in our midst.

Really, we would not consider a racial component to crime even if no white person committed a wrongdoing. Anti-white ideologies insist that no other race is guiltier of crime than we are, whatever the reality.

We do not tolerate white people's crimes as we tolerate crimes by other races. Neither does anyone else. The defences we offer other races, we do not offer our own.

When we punish ourselves, other races punish us too. While other races are furious to think we are prejudiced against them, they have no problems with their prejudices against us. Neither have we.

With our ridiculous rules about race, criminals of other races do not represent their race, but white criminals represent white people. We have no qualms about abusing white races as we do not dare defame other races.

While dismissing disproportionately high rates of crime by other races, people talk of white people committing crimes and terror at a rate that is simply untrue. In this analysis, white males commit crimes because they supposedly resent having lost power, which in the West's pursuit of equality (more fanatical than any religion) we think is desirable.

White Prejudice

To promote tolerance of other races and deal with issues of racism, we report the races of white criminals and victims of colour. Nothing is better than when they come together: white mischief.

The worst of all criminals are racist white criminals. White criminals' racism we make central to their identity, even if the crimes they commit are not against anyone of another race. We have no worries about people's prejudice against racist white people. We want it.

White racists do not need to be criminals to be treated as if they were. They need only to be racist. Never has there been an era for creating words like ours, but decades of crime and terror by other races and their religions have not allowed us words disparaging of other races or religions.

At a time when we search for reasons to avoid incarcerating most criminals, we are looking for reasons to incarcerate racists. We offer them none of the leniency we offer hoods and rapists from other races.

We cannot imagine rehabilitating white racists. Upon them, we impose exemplary punishments and damages.

Traumatic experiences excusing crime by other races do not excuse crime by racist white people. We do not indulge them their crimes or even their racism for their poverty or other problems.

Poor white people often seem sad lonely figures, estranged from everyone amidst multiculturalism, without gangs, communities, or their race to stand with them. We expect white people to embrace multiculturalism and the loss of their countries and homes, while helping other races along. If white people feel out of place amidst multiculturalism, we give them none of the sympathies we afford people of other races, not even when crime by other races led to their prejudice. We are simply not fussed about other races' crimes and bigotry.

Instead, we are consumed by hostility to white people's bigotry. People of other races are empowered to bash us not only for the racial epithets we use, but for the epithets they accuse us of using.

White Ignorance

Only a fool opens his home to someone he knows might steal his crockery. Only the naïve opens her home to strangers without contemplating they might harm her.

Imagining that a world without countries would be peaceful has proven incredibly naïve. With experience, some people once relaxed about interracial immigration have become concerned. For the most part, the West remains naïve.

The West has welcomed, respected, and embraced immigrants, but we still presume to make multiculturalism work by preventing white people's prejudice, as if the problem with racial diversity is us. That prejudice might only be our secret fears and suspicions inside Western heads, but we fret more for white people's fears than we fret for immigrants' knives.

So much as drawing a negative inference about people of another race, thinking they are anything but good (save only for that handful of individuals not as bad as we can be anyway), we dismiss for being irrational. It might be xenophobia or another of our postmodern phobias.

We do not have a word for rationally feeling heightened anxieties or anxieties at all when people of other races in general or in particular approach us, certain such anxieties can never be rational. A woman sitting in an otherwise empty railway carriage cannot let the race of the man coming towards her, his eyes set upon her, influence her decision whether to prime her telephone for a call or to guide her fingers nearer the spray in her bag.

Rhetoric cannot replace reality. It can only conceal or reveal it.

We cannot talk our way out of reality by touting bits of evidence we like and denying streams of evidence we do not. Saying people are the same does not change the differences.

We pretend we have no problems around race. Thus there is no problem to solve.

It frees up our time to deal with other people's problems. When we do acknowledge problems between other races, we imagine they can be overcome with a chat.

It is the arrogance of our ignorance, basking in our accolades while strangers tear us down. We prefer ignorance and stupidity to racism, but problems are not resolved by being ignored.

Marketing Multiculturalism

Without race to distinguish us from immigrants or to link us with our forebears, we credit immigrant races with the best of our history as we have ceased crediting ourselves. It is not true, but talk of immigrants' supposed contributions to our past justifies still more interracial immigration, shaming us out of racial resistance.

In particular, we talk up those people from other races contributing to our defence from other Europeans in war, especially the two world wars, way beyond the facts. Never does our forebears' sacrifice seem more futile, or our governments more neglectful of the people who suffered and died for us, than to read history belittle and discard our soldier, sailor, and airmen forebears, their nurses and other adjutants, while accrediting their achievements and sacrifices to others.

Multiculturalism betrays not just our descendants and compatriots. It betrays our forebears.

Most races make more of the death of one of their own than the death of anyone else. We make more of the deaths of people from other races, especially when it serves to promote tolerance and welcoming of those other races. There are deaths and relative deaths, according to whether the relatives are ours.

Most notable and pervasive among the opinions reported as facts around the ideological West are opinions enthusing for multiculturalism. Western multiculturalism founded upon ideology and naïvety is sustained by marketing and spin. Without them, there would be all sorts of dissent.

We market immigration by claiming immigrants help us, generally and in particular. Questioning multiculturalism because of particular individuals might seem spurious, but we tirelessly tout the benefits of immigration by citing individuals.

Marketing racial diversity makes immigrant success stories important to tell. Success makes their race relevant to their story, as it does not for successful white people.

Race is always relevant to stories of how good people of other races are. They cannot help but make us want more.

While refusing to generalise the bad deeds by individuals of other races to the rest of those races, we generalise the good. We generalise all immigrants to be like the best of them. We have no pretence of objectivity when complimenting other races, or complimenting ourselves for having welcomed them.

Dividing white people into those who fight racism and those who promote it, anyone who does not generalise all immigrants to be like the best of them, we assume is generalising them all to be like the worst of them. We dismiss those people for being racists.

Reports of kind refugees are not ambivalent. They are euphoric. We market asylum by claiming refugees suffered, much as they claimed to have suffered when seeking asylum, until we saved them.

Journalists taint the news of other races. News services taint their skin colours too, whitening swarthy complexions among refugees to cajole Western opinion. Christianity is never more fondly described than in articles about Christian refugees.

Normally, refugee status and race remain hidden when refugees commit crimes, but not when there is a chance to portray that refugee's suffering. Never is a murderer described in more glowing terms than when he is, or was, a refugee.

Refugee status can also be revealed by refugees suffering as a result of other refugees' crimes. It might be the pain people feel when someone of their race suffers, as we no longer feel for white people suffering. Their supposed suffering might be no more than the risk of prejudice against them, as if immigrants suffering prejudice is much worse than white people being raped or murdered.

We romanticise not just what modern-day refugees are, but what they will become: doctors, engineers, and so forth. If it ever happens, we will know. Our media will report it, over and over.

We trumpet multiculturalism as the purveyor of greatness, trying desperately to achieve our globalist ideal. Our countries might blow apart otherwise.

Lies

Early in the twenty-first century, we credited the freedom to spread information around social media with empowering Muslims to revolution from their dictatorships in North Africa and the Middle East. Meanwhile, in the West, social media companies increasingly shut down dissidents disseminating information.

Paradoxically, we blame crime by other races on social media facilitating communication among their own. We do not blame crime upon those races.

Facts are not our focus. Racial harmony is.

The overwhelming evidence of racial diversity being negative only makes seizing upon faint flickers of anything positive more important. The news is good.

If nothing is positive, we make it up. Lying never does anybody any harm lauding diversity.

Where immigrants are rife, and so crime is rife, police superiors instruct police not to record crime. Police and politicians can thus declare there is no crime, as if crime does not exist if police do not record it.

What senior police and political leaders cannot conceal, they distort. They lie.

A lack of statistics about the race and religion of criminals does not deter politicians and police spokesmen and women from lying: from insisting there is no correlation between race or religion and crime. Having statistics about the race and religion of criminals is not a reason for police commissioners to be truthful, when they are racist statistics. The truth is racist.

Junior police are more forthcoming in private conversations and anonymous social media, provided their superiors do not know. Telling the truth about race requires anonymity, in this Age of Ideology. Lying does not.

Race is not relevant to immigrant crime at the time, but it becomes relevant in the future to stories of crime being overcome. The end of crime becomes newsworthy as the crime never was. Thus police and media admit to immigrant crime in the past to say it is no longer the case, giving immigrants the credit for ending it.

The problems of multiculturalism are our fault. Overcoming those problems are the immigrants' achievements.

When police and media admit the racial bedlam, it is not the bedlam that is but the bedlam that used to be. We might acknowledge a racially troubled past, even a recent past, as we do not acknowledge a racially troubled present. While we deny race is a factor in crime and riots today, we might acknowledge race being behind past crime and riots, as we never did at the time. We think that proves race was an issue but no longer is: that time and we have overcome race.

None of it fazes us, in our merry middle-class homes. We smile and laugh, never wondering what might be coming closer towards us. Ours is the ecstasy in virtual space that people must feel when they are high on hallucinogenic drugs. The challenge is waking up in the morning.

Urban Decay

Countries, cities, and suburbs that different races occupy clearly differ in their appearances. The psychological differences between races seem to include cleanliness, public hygiene, and civic order.

When we owned our countries, we had reason to make and keep our cities beautiful. We owned them by virtue of our race. We belonged. Other races did not.

Immigrants do not feel the responsible ownership of Western countries that we used to feel. Theirs is the ownership of having received gifts, without effort on their part and nothing to value.

We feel no ownership at all, anymore. Without other races keeping streets clean, we stopped bothering.

Since World War II, the West has become a place where everyone belongs, but the problem with places where everyone belongs is that no one belongs. When everybody owns something, nobody owns it. What were English cities became nobody's cities.

Without a sense that people own something, they have no reason to maintain or improve it. In multiracial suburbs and cities, we are all tenants. No one has reason to care, not even us anymore. We employ street cleaners.

At their best, our cities are simply dirtier. We might think Western streets are clean because we compare them to the worst of the world's slums, unaware of what they were and might have remained, were they still ours.

We know only of washroom doors at petrol stations and railway stations being locked because of the risk of vandalism, opened by keys we borrow from attendants. Those doors used to be unlocked.

By any standard but a complete rejection of everything Western and embracing of everything else, our cities have markedly declined. Formerly elegant streets have become grubby and crass, crammed with Asian and African commerce of anything at all. We accept without question the Middle Eastern security guards posted around shopping centres and in hospitals, government offices, and other public places, not cognisant of never having needed them before immigrants became numerous.

We treat our countries with contempt. We can hardly expect other races to do otherwise.

At their worst, Western inner cities grand only a generation or two ago lie practically in ruin. Vast tracts of streets are unrecognisable from their images in old films.

Once impressive stone buildings now lie wrecked, with windows broken and walls fraying. They are not settings so often for films anymore, except at the extremes that make them seem distant, like comic book fantasies. Their undefined squalor makes reality around us seem better, from our distant television sets in our distant private homes.

We live our heady days of splendour in the suburbs, where conversations rarely turn to shadowy streets. They get little mention in the evening news, except as stories of renewal each time a park is laid.

More often than not, we do not think of those places. Blind that they exist, we lose them behind thick silver mirrors reflecting images of shopping malls we see. Our altogether-visions in television programmes and commercials are of sanitised streets and peaceful places, with happy people and good purchasing.

While Western cities and communities deteriorated, our impressions of them blossomed. We are not trying to improve them because we think our pretty cities cannot get any prettier. We believe the publicity: our urban illusion.

Realities of multiculturalism seemingly inescapable, we escape. That is, unless there is a means of blaming white people for what other races do. Rather than risk linking our cities' degeneration with the coming of other races, we blame governments failing to provide infrastructure, as if a few more concrete pylons could make everything all right.

Without means for blaming white people, we are compelled to blot those places from our minds, unless chance befalls us. Confronting those places risks us confronting issues of race and culture.

Considerations of civic pride and order, public health and hygiene, and cleanliness become as racist as considerations of crime and misbehaviour. Any sense that a place occupied by white people could be better than a place occupied by other races becomes prejudice.

Preferring pretty streets and cities to those sullied is labelled white supremacy, because it treats our past culture of cleanliness as better than cultures of mess and mire. Preferring buildings with windows intact to those with broken windows becomes akin to Nazism.

Weapons

Schoolyard brawls were much less dangerous when our schools were homogeneously white. When white boys fought, they fought with their fists. They wrestled.

If boys of some other races use their fists, they have wire wrapped around them. They also use weapons, including flick knives, other knives, knuckledusters, meat cleavers, broken glass bottles, machetes, baseball bats, extendable batons, throwing stars, and electric shock devices. Among their more resourceful weapons are bicycle chains, tyre levers, clubs, and bedposts.

They are weapons for people without firearms. Many have firearms.

In our raceless and cultureless vision of the world, people of other races do not kill. Knives, guns, alcohol, and males do.

Women have also come to fight. If white women have not learnt to fight from women of other races fighting, they learnt it from being told they could do everything men do.

When we are around other races not shy to use weapons, we cannot remain oblivious to weaponry as we remain oblivious to race. Multiculturalism compels white people to take up arms they otherwise would not.

So does individualism. Western countries without need or thought to restrict gun ownership do so not just because other races use guns, but because we without nationalism and other senses of community use guns too. It happened in the American Wild West after the destruction of Southern society with the Civil War. It happens whenever we lose nationalist unity.

At best, immigration eventually transforms our countries into the countries from which the immigrants came. They are the reason those countries from which immigrants came were like that.

At worst, our countries become worse than those countries of origin. People left behind in their countries have some sense of society. They possess their countries, so have reason to care about them. They do not possess ours, not yet.

Community Conflict

Criminals from other races are more likely than white people to enjoy organisations to support and protect them, as well as harm them. They also have their communities.

White criminals normally act alone. White people are individuals.

People of other races are more likely to act collectively, because they think collectively. They retain their familial, tribal, and racial loyalties we rarely recognise.

Nevertheless, we treat criminals of other races as individuals, without reference to their race. Anything else might lead to negative generalisations about their race or about racial diversity generally.

Only good people from other races we call their communities, because we like positive generalisations about other races. Other races do not make that distinction. From their viewpoints, theirs are communities, whatever the contexts.

Their communities safeguard them all from wrongdoers within their race and without. When someone from their race is the victim and the wrongdoer is from another race, their loyalty is to the victim. When the victims of wrongdoing are from other races, without harm to their race or anyone of it, then their loyalty is to the wrongdoer.

They might be victims of no more than rudeness or abuse. Rather than being so rude or racist as to mention people of other races' rudeness to us, we accept their improprieties against us. Other races do not accept improprieties against them.

The West responded to racial conflict by abandoning our race. Other races respond by affirming theirs.

Conflict might arise from misunderstanding: an ill-considered glance; a wrong choice of word. It might arise from no more than people of different races wanting the same thing: a place on a park bench, perhaps. Defying someone from their race means defying their race, as we can no longer conceive. Conflict might arise from perceptions of their power and influence across a country or across a school canteen.

Social breakdown necessitates the growth of gangs. Criminal gangs are the most violent expression of people's tribal natures, even if they first draw members wanting the lifestyle or money. They are not joining to be individuals, but for belonging and power. Gangs have the same disinterest in people outside their gangs that races have in other races and individuals have in everyone.

Gangs are typically based upon race, even if we refuse to recognise it because those gangs are criminal. If they were sociable or charitable, we would happily recognise their racial foundations.

Those gangs are not white. The faceless flash mobs periodically terrorising American cities are not mobs of white people.

When circumstances compel us to recognise criminals of other races acting collectively, then we do so for their excuse. While we tell our children that other children being naughty is no excuse for them being naughty too, gang membership can alleviate punishments for other races.

Racial Conflict

Races fight each other all over the world. Tribes of the same race fight each other, especially in Africa and the Middle'East. They fight each other outside the West and continue fighting each other within Western countries, often more so because we bring them in close proximity to each other with the liberties we grant them.

We equate prejudice with conflict, but when we face racial or religious prejudice manifest in conflict, we consider only the conflict. Political, economic, and other class warfare we find acceptable discussion points: colourless conflict. Fixated with racial and religious harmony, we are uninterested in other harmony.

Racial and religious feuds we do not discuss. We do not conceive racial blame upon other races as we do upon white people.

When immigrants attack each other, we do not criticise either race. Instead, we work hard to soothe racial divisions. We rattle off more accolades for the strengths of diversity, but if our accolades for diversity are not to convince other races, then they are to convince white people.

In our hostility to racism, news services report a criminal's racial hatred, whatever his race. The criminal not being white, his race remains irrelevant. If that unfairly maligns white people and especially white racists for crimes committed by people of other races, then nobody cares.

Unlike white people, the crimes engaging other races' interests are not those in which people of their race are the wrongdoers, but those in which people from their race are the victims. They, including those in their homelands and other countries, express racial solidarity inconceivable to us.

With news services omitting mention of a criminal's race, people in other countries are liable to blame white people for crimes committed in Western countries. Thus their racial solidarity with immigrant victims of crime becomes more hostility towards white people.

Immigrants living in Western countries close to the crime scenes know better. White people have learnt not to notice the race of people attacking us, but other races do not yield to our ideologies of indifference. They have their experiences and no reticence in identifying the race of people attacking them. The criminals attacking them are not white.

We have no bar of their racism. We defend other races being criticised for crime whatever the critics' race, as we do not defend our race.

Being blind to race but not racism, we take responsibility for other races' racism. Noticing that the crimes and racism against immigrants for which we are so ashamed are not committed by white people would be racist.

Our vicarious culpability for other races' crimes committed in our countries is not a national culpability we carry. It is racial. We do not impose it upon Western citizenry of other races.

White Flight

Our countries were gentler, more peaceful places when they were ours. Within Western cities, we were once free to move around. We strolled, even promenaded, smiling at strangers we passed. We conversed with unfamiliar strangers on a bus.

When people of other races came to our countries, cities, and neighbourhoods, we welcomed them, but white societies that survived small numbers of people from other races have not survived large enough numbers for them to become their own communities. Our lives deteriorated, most notably with social isolation and crime. Sooner or later, we moved away.

The phrase "white flight" describes the people who fled those streets, suburbs, and cities. It became expressive of white people's supposed intolerance and racism rather than the disaster that diversity proved to be, but not only white people fled.

Other races in their countries have not welcomed immigrants as we have. There has thus been no black, brown, or yellow flight like white flight.

Large numbers of crimes are no longer reported to police. Other crimes are averted because white people, especially elderly white people, women, and children, are confined to their homes. We have become wary.

Having become racially diverse, or devoid of white people altogether, streets and suburbs where once we walked, we no longer walk. We are victims of crime and would be victims more often, but we are too scared to venture outside at night and are careful where we go by day.

We now close ourselves in small places, shut off from everyone else. In private clubs and gated communities, seclusion is isolation.

It is hard not to contemplate there would be less crime without the races we have allowed to share our cities and countries, that we would feel safer leaving our homes and venturing outside or into other suburbs were our neighbourhoods still ours, but we do not cater to white people's fears. We call them phobias, however rational they are.

That does not keep people of other races claiming a phobia when they are suing us for compensation because of crime by other races still. They can have their fears because of multiculturalism, and be paid money in compensation. We are not trying to silence them by declaring their fears of other races irrational.

Balkanisation

The West giving up our collective territorial rights allows other races to assert their territorial interests in our place. Balkanisation refers to the division of a country or region into unco-operative or even belligerent smaller countries or regions. The term was first applied to divisions by race and religion when Muslim Turks invaded the Balkan Peninsular. With the collapse of the Ottoman and Russian Empires after World War I, the term came into more common use.

The term ought to have been mentioned more often through the collapse of communist dictatorship and the dissolution of Yugoslavia in 1991, but we had stopped recognising race and religion by then. It is applicable to anywhere multiracial.

Removing formal borders between races around the West led to informal borders between races. Structured segregation gave way to unstructured segregation. Free market demographics means other races stake out territories we dare not breach.

We accept whole streets, suburbs, and cities we can no longer enter. Rather than label those areas by the races or religion that now occupy them, we euphemistically call them urban areas or sensitive urban areas, but we could wander there safely when they were our urban areas.

If we venture there and suffer, we blame ourselves for having been so silly as to go there. White people always blame ourselves, rather than be so racist as to blame people of another race for anything.

Police know where not to go, or not to go alone. Before entering some immigrant areas, police need permission from immigrant community leaders: those races' de facto authorities. Like other failings of multiculturalism, police are prone to deny needing such permission rather than admit publicly to racial caution.

Each race's precincts are not just dangerous for white people. They are dangerous for people from other races. We are all to keep to our precincts.

Other races but ours create criminal domains. The streets become ever more dangerous.

Warnings

Informing the public what races and religions proportionately more often commit domestic violence, rape, murder, other crimes, and terrorism might warn people of dangers. It might protect them from loss, harm, or death. So too might informing the public if particular races are more likely to carry particular communicable diseases.

Interestingly, authorities make sporadic exemptions to warn us about gypsies, taking food, money, and other items as they do, quite apart from other crimes they commit. That might be because we do not realise gypsies are a race, or because they are gypsies.

Our reticence about mentioning race allows problems to fester, which only bothers us when the vulnerable races are not ours. We will warn people of other races of the dangers they face, from their own or from others, as we do not warn white people.

Other races are not so cruel to their own as we are to ours. They care for their kind. They warn their people to keep away from particular races and neighbourhoods, or from immigrant areas of the West altogether, as we dare not, not publicly. Policemen who privately warn us not to enter immigrant areas add the proviso that they will deny their warnings if they are quoted.

While parents of other races warn their children of the problems of other races, we do not. That would be racist.

Warning black children about white people's alleged racism is politically acceptable. Warning other people's children about black crime is not.

Protecting our children's lives demands we teach them to act safely, taking precautions, knowing where the risks of harm most likely lie, but we are supposed to teach them paying no regard to race or religion. We demonise discrimination and carry on regardless.

Withholding facts from children for their sake allows children their childhoods: imaginations of a world that is not, in visions better for being unreal. They suffer no harm, while the day will come they will be old enough for the truth.

Denying our children knowledge of reality for our sake and for the sake of our ideological dreams is child abuse. We cast visions becoming dangerous for being untrue, from which we never want them old enough for the truth.

Refusing to teach our children the truth about race and religion, ours is a conspiracy of silence and falsehood. We inculcate our children with our ideals for what we wish the world was.

They listen faithfully unaware that the truth is something else altogether, hidden far behind our smiles. Bleaching their minds with multicultural lies, we leave them vulnerable to harm, even death.

Prejudice

Military interests justify particular racial discriminations. Might other national, social, familial, and personal interests also justify particular discriminations?

Every instance we learn the race or religion of a criminal, we have knowledge from which we can learn. We might have cause to wonder whether our personal security demands that we watch warily that darker-skinned stranger, rather than inviting him home for some tea.

Acknowledging racial reality that we refuse to acknowledge, people of other races are often wary of people of particular races, even their own race, as we cannot imagine. We are only wary of white people.

Prejudice can be rational, based upon knowledge and experience. Trust can be irrational, based upon ignorance and misconception. Trust is never more irrational than it is when it is based upon ideology.

We insist that racism hurts, but racism does not hurt people saved from harm by racism: theirs or anyone else's. Racism saves people.

If people of some races and religions are more criminal, diseased, or otherwise more dangerous to be around than people of other races and religions, then the people blithely trusting those people are not simply naïve. They are victims of cruel and culpable propaganda.

We would rather suffer crime or contract communicable disease, or at least let other people suffer crime or contract communicable disease, than discriminate on the grounds of race or religion, or be seen to discriminate on the grounds of race or religion. We refuse to be racist, without caring about the consequences of our refusal.

Our rejection of racism condemns us and other people to harm. White people have suffered and died trusting they had no reason to fear people of other races and religions.

Dangers make some prejudice desirable. Racial and religious prejudice saves people's lives.

Withholding facts about races and cultures kills people. Not everyone is willing to be a martyr for multiculturalism: dying knowing that she is not racist in the people against whom she takes precautions.

Our compatriots have lives like ours, but we do not care if all of them suffer or die, provided we do not discriminate. Multiculturalism is evil.

Multiculturalism and Individualism

However much the noble and ignoble wish otherwise, multiculturalism fails because it is predicated upon individualism: people not becoming involved when someone of their race or religion feels offended, mistreated, hurt, or killed. Only white people buy into it.

Multiculturalism depends upon white people's disregard for other white people's well-being: our individualism. Multiculturalists are individualists: that reverse face of the same ideological coin. Other races now harm us with our concurrence.

All our lauding of immigration and racial integration cannot detract from the fact that there would be white people alive and unharmed if we had not allowed other races to immigrate, but we do not care enough about them, if we care about them at all. We are more interested in the immigrants and their children whose lives are better and might have been saved because we did welcome them. They are the people upon whom we pride ourselves.

Without seeing our bloody hands for crimes that immigrants commit and the suffering they wilfully or inadvertently inflict, our embrace of racial and religious diversity matters more than human life matters, even thousands or millions of human lives matter, even our lives matter. We are taking exacting and extraordinary measures to console and cajole each other through interracial immigration, no matter who suffers and dies.

No number of immigrants talking about race, even scrawling their hatred of white people across our monuments, keeps us from smugly insisting that race is not real, that all races are equal, or that our problem is white people's prejudice. We will keep insisting so when they slash *"kill whitey"* across our pale sorry faces. If we are not willing to die and to let our families and races die in the name of diversity, then we cannot be completely committed to multiculturalism.

The Loneliest People on Earth

A few generations ago, we had countries, races, and families. We cared about each other as compatriots did, rather than fretting about everyone else. We now look back with horror we did.

Immigrants are at the forefront not just of celebrating multiculturalism but our other national celebrations too. Multiculturalism is premised upon us making other races, not white people, feel welcome. To that end, we push white people from view.

Not everyone belongs, after all. While other races can talk of their race, country, and heritage, we cannot talk of ours. Still we persevere, whatever circumstances befall us. We keep moving along, trying to get through the weeks as well as we can.

Multiracial places are no places for individuals. They are worst for people brave enough to be heroes.

We thus taper our dealings with other races. White boys at school do not bully boys of other races for fear of being taken aside for racism. They bully other white boys.

White people are our citizens of the world, without countries to keep us or a people to care. Western individuals are abjectly vulnerable, without a race in which to believe or history to hold, at least that anyone wants. We have our rights, but they are rights we can no longer exercise. Rights do not make people smile.

We might consider ourselves to have a community, but our communities are small, without the powerful or rich. We have no government to call on for anything but money, as everybody can, but never anywhere near enough. The West that could have cared for us has the world for which to worry: every human being and even plants and animals to help.

Knowing what white people think about race, our decline, and the changes under way across the homeless West is difficult. We confine our complaints and other racism to private conversations with people we know and others we presume will not damn us for naughty thoughts and feelings. White people have become the saddest, loneliest people on earth.

Questioning Multiculturalism

There is every good reason to make the best of life by seeing the positives in things we cannot change. We see only the benefits of racial diversity because we feel we have no choice but to accept it, but our inviolate presumption was not one our forebears made, the rest of the world makes, or interracial immigrants make about the countries they or their forebears left behind.

Ours are the democracies of the world, in which we consent to being powerless. If we imagine being empowered, if only in the sanctuary of our minds, then we can question whether the West needs multiculturalism, or wants it.

We could resume telling the truth about race and racial diversity. We could let others tell the truth. We could allow the inquiries, discussion, and debate about race and culture that we and others have spent decades suppressing.

For all their cries, if we really believed the problems of indigenous races were our fault because colonial Europeans came (but not the fault of recent immigrants because we had already come), then we would denote their tribal homelands national borders and all head our separate ways. We do not. Instead, we do whatever is simplest for us to assist them.

We dream that if only we could overcome white people's supposed racism, then everything would be grand, but anyone believing white racism denies other races jobs, housing, and other services should welcome racially dedicated states, as states remain outside the West. So keen are we to aid other races, white people could send money over borders and visit other countries to help. We do now.

To think other white people are our responsibility would be racism. That would also make our well-being their responsibility.

All cultures are not equal, least of all for people who have suffered because of particular cultures. Our forebears suffered. Our compatriots suffer. Our descendants will suffer.

Unravelling Multiculturalism

Our cities and countries are hopelessly divided by race and by culture. When white people mention it, we accuse them of being divisive. When other races mention it, we thank them for bringing it to our attention. We try to do better.

No other race has welcomed immigrants as the West has done. No other race has attempted multiculturalism of the kind we have. For that, immigrants still keep telling us that we have failed: that we are racist; that our countries and our political, judicial, school, and all other systems remain racist. The more we admit immigrants from other races, the more we are accused of racism.

Rather than imagine that we and our compatriots are not racist, we find reasons to think that refugees and other immigrants have no choice but to come to our countries and stay, although it means they must suffer our racism. It is not true.

Ought we not just raise our hands and admit that we failed? We can say we are sorry, we tried our best, but we simply cannot make multiculturalism work.

Occasionally, some Western countries have toyed with gently undoing our multiracial experiment, again respecting human nature rather than denying or trying to change human nature. Being so gentle, little happened.

Undoing multiculturalism will first require us to re-join the rest of the world in racial self-belief and loyalty: caring for others among our race, especially our descendants. Racism, nationalism, and discrimination can be rational, when it is in favour of our own, not against our own.

Normally people pay a price for a country, but immigrants enjoy residence in our lands because we gave it to them. What we gave, we can recover.

We have come to disavow notionally democratic governments when they embark upon wars with which we disagree, turn away immigrants we would admit, or expel people we would allow to remain. We could just as easily disavow our governments for having admitted immigrants we did not authorise them to admit, rescinding those immigrants' purported permission to stay.

The governments who gave our countries away never asked us whether they could give them away. Our countries were not theirs to give.

We might not need to deport anyone. We might need only to remove the financial, cultural, political, and other inducements we provide people of other races to come into our countries and to stay: the free or subsidised education and healthcare; the payments of pensions and welfare; the jobs; our submission to their cultural desires; the rights to vote in our elections. We might need only to discriminate in favour of our race, as other races discriminate in favour of their race.

The past cannot change. The future can.

The longer we take before unravelling our multiracial experiment, restoring our countries, the more difficult it will be. The more costly it will have been.

APPENDIX:
THE STRUGGLE BETWEEN RACES

In spite of white people's propensity for helping other races, Englishman Charles Darwin wrote in 1859 of the struggles for existence between individuals and between races. We struggle for anything we value.

Primitive tribespeople valued their existence: their tribes. They thus valued food, water, and security.

As they developed, tribes increasingly valued their cultures, especially their religions. They valued material things.

That struggle became racial and other tribal tension, whenever different races and other tribes became close. Often, that tension breaks into conflict, especially where resources they all value are limited.

None of our touting of immigration diminishes the real reasons the West began welcoming so many immigrants from other races through the second half of the twentieth century: fundamentally, because it is against our national interests. We do not want nations anymore.

Without collective identities, there can be no collective conflict, no countries to combat, we think. Without nations there would be no wars between nations, but losing our nations does not mean there are no wars. It means we lack a means of defending ourselves.

Racial and cultural struggles, tensions, and conflicts did not cease because the West refuses to recognise race and culture, especially religion. They are simply conflicts that white people, in pursuit of peace, however painful that peace, refuse to fight.

Defending our race would be racist, when we are resolutely determined not to be racist, too frightened to be racist. Instead, we submit, in the face of racial abuse and attacks against us.

Racial tension, conflict, and war are natural whenever different races live in close proximity to each other. White people battling our own is unnatural.

More divisive than race is our rejection of racism. When faced with a racially charged conflict involving white people, or even a whiff of white racism in the air, we side with other races against our own, not in spite of their race but because of it.

There is more than enough tension and conflict when different races come together, without white people adding tension and conflict between us. Refusing to fight other races, we turn our hostility towards our own.

We of the West no longer value our race, countries, or cultures. We value only our individual selves.

Naïvely taking food and water for granted, we value money and spending it, in this Age of Money. We value multiculturalism, in this Age of Ideology.

The Age of Ideology is the age in which ideological conflicts mask racial and cultural conflicts, for a West immersed in ideology but denying ourselves race and culture. Even individualism is essentially a racial conflict. It is promoted by those from outside our race wanting to weaken and isolate us, separating us from our race and culture. It is promoted by those inside our race wanting to separate themselves from their race or culture, or opposing their race for some personal immoral return.

Nationalism and other tribalism is our rejection of individualism. It is our defence from anyone or anything harming us. It is our support in our struggles for existence.

Other races care little about ideas and even less about ideologies. They care about race, culture, and heritage: theirs.

Conflicts will increase between immigrant races as their numbers grow. White people desperate for peace and harmony will not know which way to kneel. We will clamour for dialogue between races, while nobody listens.

Communism

In the nineteenth century, Karl Marx on the face of it interpreted history as a struggle between social and economic classes. That belied the racial and religious struggle at the core of Marx's family experience: irreligious Jews living in Lutheran Prussia.

Behind the efforts to strip people of race, culture, and countries, communism began as essentially a racial struggle between irreligious Jews and Europeans. Disillusioned Europeans, most notably Marx's Prussian collaborator and benefactor Friedrich Engels, sided with irreligious Jews against their race.

Communism was also a cultural conflict, hostile to Western culture and thus Christianity. It was similarly hostile to Judaism and, initially, other religions.

The Russian Empire was the setting of several pogroms against Jews, before being ravaged by the Great War. Mother Russia collapsed into revolution in March 1917.

While Marx seventy years earlier had presumed the inevitability of communism, the mixed-race Vladimir Ulyanov (better known as Lenin) believed that advancing the communist cause required violence. Even if the imposition of communism did not require violence, then it justified violence. Marxism became Marxist-Leninism, even if Leninism became rarely mentioned. The political struggle became killing and war.

Violence was at the forefront of communist revolution and invasion. Amidst a second Russian revolution, in November 1917, the communist Bolsheviks took power, precipitating civil war.

Despite the last Russian tsar, Nicholas II, having abdicated sixteen months earlier, communists murdered the Russian royal family, including children, along with their friends and servants in July 1918. They murdered Russia.

Amidst the breakdown of civilisation and confidence in the European order because of the Great War, several revolutions broke out across Europe from 1917. The Bolshevik Revolution precipitated a wave of expressly communist revolutions across Europe until 1923. All the communist revolutions, bar the Bolshevik Revolution, ultimately failed.

The Communist Empire

Exiting the Great War, Soviet Russia signed the Treaty of Brest–Litovsk with Germany, Austria–Hungary, Bulgaria, and the Ottoman Empire in March 1918. Muslim Turks broke the treaty by invading Christian Armenia in May of that year. Later that year, Soviet Russia also reneged.

Marxists promptly embarked upon more war, wherever they thought they would win. Waging war when the rest of Europe found armistice, Soviet Russia attacked Estonia, Belarus, Ukraine, and Poland in an offensive aiming to make Europe communist by invasion or revolution. Poland thwarted it in 1921.

Through the Russian Civil War across much of what had been the Russian Empire, Belarus and Ukraine both lost to the Bolsheviks. They became the Belarusian and Ukrainian Soviet Socialist Republics in January and February 1919.

Russian communists intervened in Muslim Azerbaijan making it a Soviet Republic in April 1920. They invaded Christian Armenia and Christian Georgia, making them Soviet Republics in December 1920 and February 1921. They reconstituted Transcaucasia as the Transcaucasian Socialist Federative Soviet Republic in March 1922.

Communists united Russia, Belarus, Ukraine, and Transcaucasia in a communist superstate, the Soviet Union, in December 1922. Behind the rhetoric, the superstate was Russia restoring her empire over other races. Behind that racial empire was the racial empire of communism: irreligious Jews and disillusioned Europeans ruling Russians and others.

The Soviet Union became, in essence, imperial Russia, but without belief in being Russian. It was Russia without Russian Orthodox Christianity and the rest of Russian culture. It was Russia, without Russia.

In economic terms, communism was a command economy, centralising power and decision making. In political terms, it was a totalitarian dictatorship, much as Lenin more than Marx had envisaged. More pragmatic than the idealistic Marx had been, Lenin realised that only a totalitarian dictatorship could hold a multiracial superstate together. The Soviet Union was a communist empire.

Joseph Stalin

Following the death of revolutionary leader Vladimir Lenin in 1924, the ideological split within Soviet communism between Joseph Stalin, an irreligious Georgian, and Leon Trotsky, an irreligious Jew, was essentially one between the disillusioned Europeans and the irreligious Jews. Stalin's rise as dictator reflected an immediate focus upon cementing socialism in one country, the Soviet Union, there being no other communist countries with which to rally. Trotsky's worldwide ambitions were more immediately globalist in reach.

While Stalin was not Russian, most powerful people in the Soviet Union were. Soviet authorities sought to erase racial loyalties and nationalism to meld people into a new super-nationalism, a forerunner to globalism. Soviet citizens were supposedly not Russian, Ukrainian, or Belarusian, nor Armenian, Georgian, or Azerbaijani in Transcaucasia, let alone any other race and nationality within Soviet borders for which no republic was named. They were not Christian, Muslim, or Jew, in a superstate seeking to erase religion as much as overcome race.

For all its ideological rejection of racism, the Soviet Union suffered conflicts racial in nature, most profoundly affecting Ukraine, the second largest republic after Russia. While other races were also affected and not all Ukrainians were, the Soviet famines of 1932 and '33 disproportionately affected the restive Ukrainians. From three to twelve million Ukrainians died during the Holodomor famine.

The communists might have insisted there was no racial aspect to the famine, but they denied orchestrating the famine altogether. Ukrainians recognised its racial component, against them.

Estimates vary widely, but in pursuit of power and implementing communist ideology disenfranchising races stronger than his own, Stalin killed somewhere between five and seventy million Russians, Ukrainians, and others, almost all of them white, from 1924 until his death in 1953. The most commonly cited total is around about twenty million dead.

Ideology masks individual self-interest. By the late 1930s, massacring the Soviet military and other elite in defence of his personal power was at the cost of the Soviet Union's defence when Nazi Germany attacked it in 1941. There was no greater individualist than Stalin.

Without the Soviet or Transcaucasian superstate, Stalin might still have been a murderous tyrant, but he might have killed only Georgians. The Soviet superstate allowed him to spread tyranny and death far and wide. Superstates do.

Fascism

The first Fascists were Italian nationalists in 1919, responding to the growing threat of communism, then known as Bolshevism. While communism grew through the 1920s and '30s, so did fascism.

While other nationalists remained rattled by the Great War, fascists expressed a patriotic fervour that other Europeans had lost. They unabashedly revered their national military forces, upon which their compatriots felt too pained to dwell. They espoused authoritarianism, structure, and discipline that most people practiced more gently.

Most fascists, like many communists, were peaceful. Not harming other races or countries but defending their own, most fascists did not want war or conflict. Nor would they surrender their races, cultures, and countries to communism without it.

Fascists could be totalitarian or not, socialist or not, anti-Semitic or not. Aside from Nazism in Germany, fascism was less concerned with Jews in general than with communists in particular, for explicitly threatening their races and nations.

Totalitarian socialism with nationalism was an example of fascism. Totalitarian socialism without nationalism was, in essence, communism.

Their willingness to recourse to fighting set fascists aside from other nationalists, but made the totalitarian fascists among them seem mirror images of communists and other combatants. While communists fought against countries, races, and cultures, fascists were willing to fight and often fought in defence of their countries, races, and cultures.

In terms of being a racial struggle, Marxists were still the irreligious Jews and disillusioned Europeans. Fascists were among the Europeans not disillusioned.

Nazism

The National Socialist German Workers' Party, the Nazi Party, was totalitarian, socialist, and anti-Semitic. Unlike other fascism, the core of Nazism was a racial conflict between Germans and Jews, without thought of religion.

Adolf Hitler, Germany's Nazi chancellor from 1933 and dictator from 1934, maligned communism and international capitalism as inventions of Jews. That might have been the reason he fought communism and international capitalism. It might have been the reason he fought Jews; in effect, Nazism treated all Jews as being complicit in the communist threat. It might not have been either.

Through the 1930s, many Europeans admired Herr Hitler rebuilding his broken country. An animal lover and decorated Great War hero, the immigrant from Austria returned to Germans their self-respect, which their Great War losses gutted and the last of which we beat out of them at Versailles in 1919, and which their many achievements through the time of the Weimar Republic never healed.

Hitler was proving to be one of the two political leaders best able to bring his people out of the Great Depression. The other was the similarly admired Franklin Delano Roosevelt in democratic nationalist America.

Their means of doing so were much the same. They built highways and national infrastructure creating wealth. They were nationalists, supporting their rich and poor people, inspiring their countries and races.

With historical hindsight, the differences between the two men seem massive. They seemed much less at the time.

At the time, some critics called Roosevelt a fascist. Other critics called him a communist.

Had Hitler died then, he might have entered history as among the greatest leaders any country had seen, for what he had accomplished through his short years in power. The disenfranchising of Jews and their exodus elsewhere might have mattered no more than had previous pogroms in Russia. We would have regretted the missed opportunity of all he could have gone onto achieve.

Before Britain imagined another war with Germany (let alone the Holocaust), a renegade British voice (a drunkard and womaniser, no less) spoke of the danger Nazi Germany posed. Had we the lexicon then that we have developed of late, we would have called Winston Churchill a bigot or Naziphobe: the paranoid, lunatic fringe. Being old and from the Conservative Party, he was yesterday's man.

Hitler did not die then. Instead, Churchill entered history as among the world's great leaders.

Almost a century later, his war against Nazi Germany did not free Churchill from criticism for being a white supremacist. Churchill was comfortably, unashamedly British.

World War II and Fascism

The Russian and Spanish Civil Wars having been smaller wars between communists and nationalists, we are told that World War II was our war against fascism in essentially our first great war of ideology, but fascism had little to do with our reasons for war. Fascist dictatorships in Spain and Portugal remained neutral through World War II. We left them alone.

Winston Churchill had long recognised that the same problems in different countries required different solutions. In the 1920s and '30s, he supported fascism in Italy and Spain in defence from communism, given their circumstances, while steadfastly opposing fascism in Britain where communism was not a threat.

Implicitly, Churchill recognised that the ideal political system for European peoples is generally a classic liberal democracy. If classic liberal democracy is not available at a particular time and place or seems like it is coming under threat, then fascism is better than communism or rule by other races.

Churchill defended British interests as he saw them. He did not intervene in other countries where Britain had no interest.

Through the 1930s, before war broke out, the communist Soviet Union attempted to form an anti-fascist alliance with Western powers. We rebuffed it.

Fascism encompassed a country defending and asserting her national interests with force, if necessary. It was no reason for war by other countries, which by going to war would also be defending and asserting their national interests by force.

Other countries' militarism and imperialism are reasons to fear them only when they threaten us. Whether fascist, communist, or anything else, the political and economic systems of races and countries threatening us are immaterial.

Later in the twentieth century, fascism in Spain, Portugal, and arguably countries of Latin America gave way to returns to democracy, when the threats of communism had passed. With peace instead of World War II and when in time the threats of communism had passed, surely fascism in Germany, Italy, and

Hungary would have also given way to returns to classic liberal democracy. German culture owed more to Immanuel Kant than an Austrian corporal.

World War II and Race

Britain has long fought wars against Continental European powers too dominant. Before the twentieth century, those wars were often against France. Early in the twentieth century, those wars were against Germany.

World War II was another racial conflict. Australia's prime minister was quite explicit about our war in defence from Japan. We fought and died to defend our imperishable traditions, keeping Australia as a citadel for the British-speaking race and a place where civilisation would persist. He was a racist, as the Japanese and everybody else were too.

Keeping Australia home, our country was our defence. Our nationalism was us defending ourselves and our civilisation.

After perhaps initially being sympathetic to Nazism as another defence from communism, Winston Churchill came to see Nazism as a threat to Britain that other fascism was not. It would have been immaterial to Churchill that Adolf Hitler did not want war with Britain. Churchill believed that a strengthening Germany threatened Britain as other strengthening fascist countries did not.

World War II did not begin in Europe until Germany's expansion reached beyond Czechoslovakia into Poland and threatened to continue. It was another war defending our countries, cultures, and Europe. Germany wanted to save us from Russians, communists, and Jews. Much as we had done in the Great War, Britain wanted to save us from Germany.

Germans hated the French who forced through the gruelling punishment of Germany in the Treaty of Versailles in 1919, but did not hate the British. Among the many reasons for Nazi Germany's defeat in World War II was Hitler's apparent refusal to kill the British soldiers fleeing Dunkirk in 1940 and his refusal to invade Britain early in the war. He tried to keep peace with Britain.

When that failed, the man who waged total war against other races waged reluctant war against Britain. That reluctant war became crueller and more complete the angrier Hitler became.

At the time, Hitler was to World War II what Kaiser Wilhelm II had been to World War I. Both men were propaganda pieces: bogeymen personifying enemies, embodiments of nations.

In World War I, Germans were the Hun or the Boche. In World War II, they were Nazis. The name Nazis invited their enemies to use it.

Nazism was the latest manifestation of Germany defending and asserting her national interests with force. So did the Soviet Union and we.

World War II and Communism

Late in August 1939, the Soviet Union and Nazi Germany signed a non-aggression pact, by which they divided Poland between them. Germany invaded western Poland on the first day of September 1939. The Soviet Union invaded eastern Poland sixteen days later. Had the Soviet Union invaded Poland before Germany invaded her, instead of sixteen days afterwards, we would have declared war on the Soviet Union instead of on Germany.

Communists had no problem with countries invading Poland. Nor did communists have a problem with Nazis following that non-aggression pact, until Nazi Germany revoked the pact by invading the Soviet Union in June 1941.

The communists did not fight Nazi Germany to liberate anyone. Before entering Warsaw in 1944, Soviet troops waited while Poles and Germans killed each other.

At the Yalta Conference in February 1945, Joseph Stalin pledged to Britain and America to allow free elections in Poland after Germany's defeat. The Polish government-in-exile in London would return to Poland.

Instead, Stalin installed a puppet communist regime in Poland, as he installed puppet communist regimes throughout the territories he took. The Soviet Union conquered Eastern Europe through World War II, as Soviet Russia had failed to do after World War I.

Evicting Germany from France and other countries wreaked more death and destruction than Germany had wreaked in conquering them. By the time of Germany's surrender in May 1945 and Japan's surrender in August 1945, we were all too weak from war to continue.

Bloodied by two world wars, we had no more mood to fight and die. We had won our wars and stopped fighting. We had lost our wars and stopped fighting.

If Britain declared war on Germany in 1939 to keep Poland free, then the war in Europe was a failure. Poland would not be free until communism collapsed there in 1989. If we presumed Poland's freedom was ours, we were wrong.

World War II Redefined in Retrospect

Amidst World War II, the Holocaust was a racial war primarily, but not only, between Germans and Jews. Only a small proportion of Germans participated, but most wars are led by a small proportion of the people concerned. No war has provoked a more devastating response, not just for Germans but for all European races.

No longer is World War II the war that it was at the time: defending our countries, races, and Europe. With revelations near the end of the war of the Holocaust, World War II became the war redefined in retrospect: our retrospective war not against Germany and Japan but against Nazism. What was a racial war much like any other in nature, if not in extent and destruction, became in retrospect for much of the West an ideological war, for people becoming immersed in ideology.

Underlying that ideological war, the racial war remains. West Europeans all side with Jews. Germans now side with Jews against their forebears.

In Asia, World War II remains a racial war. The enemy of other Asians was still Japan and Japanese.

World War II became the West's definitive war: the war upon which we dwell (if we dwell upon any), as if there has never been another, although we dwell only upon the war in Europe. The newsreels that motivated us onward through the last weeks of the war still motivate us. We have become trapped in our reconstruction of the war: transfixed by the sight of Jews near death at Bergen–Belsen in April 1945.

The cries of millions of Jews through the Holocaust consume us more than do the cries of millions of Germans and millions of other Europeans who died through the gruelling four-year hell of

World War I and gruelling six-year hell of World War II. Our other enemies in those wars, most pointedly Japan who more cruelly attacked and killed us in World War II than did Germany through either war, ceased being our enemies.

No longer do we view World War II or the rest of our history from the viewpoint of our forebears, but from the viewpoint of Jewry. No other actions by totalitarian Nazi Germany, not her other wars or even her war against us, matter as does her war against the Jews.

Our redefined war is against not just Nazism, but against any sense by which white people might want to harm Jews. It is a retrospective war against prejudice but only white people's prejudice, without imagining that prejudice might ever be justified, because the Holocaust could never be justified. It is a war against racism, but only white people's racism.

Were Japan to repeat its World War II aggression and atrocities against us today, our police authorities would worry about racism. Instead of declaring war on Japan, our governments would declare war on xenophobia. Instead of fighting Japanese soldiers, our militaries would recruit them.

The Cold War

World War II left the communist Soviet Union the dominant power in Continental Europe, subjugating Eastern Europe from 1945. It became Britain's enemy.

From soon after World War II until 1991, the Cold War was presented to us as a conflict between communism and capitalism. The Soviet Union and its East European communist satellites stood on one side. Democratic America and her West European allies stood on the other.

Without anybody saying so, at least not loudly, the Cold War was a racial conflict. The free West spoke of Russia as if she were synonymous with the Soviet Union. Russia spoke of America, to mean white America.

Behind that conflict stirred the same racial conflict that underpinned communism. Throughout the free West, siding with Russia were irreligious Jews and disillusioned Europeans sympathetic to communism.

During the Cold War, communists took power in a handful of countries outside the West. They typically did so with some degree of support from the Soviet Union.

Estimates of the numbers of Chinese and others killed by communist dictator Mao Zedong from 1949 until his death in 1976 vary widely. The most commonly cited total is around forty million dead.

From 1975 until '79, dictator Pol Pot (born Saloth Sar, who had studied radio electronics in France in his youth) sought to create a perfect agrarian communist state in Cambodia. Communists murdered anyone tainted with the old order of capitalism, including those close to Western interests. Again estimates vary widely, but over the four years of the Khmer Rouge regime, executions and government policies probably killed a quarter of the Cambodian population, if not more.

Outside the West and Soviet Union, communism remained nationalist and racist, even while killing much of its race and nation in pursuit of a new communist race and nation. Everything remained nationalist and racist, outside the West and Soviet Union.

China had long sought imperial control of Tibet. Soon after communists took power in China in 1949, communist China invaded.

The Pol Pot Cambodian regime targeted ethnic Chinese, Vietnamese, and Laotians, along with intellectuals and disabled people. Chinese had been disproportionately shopkeepers.

Two countries being communist was no reason for them not to fight each other. Communist China and communist Vietnam fought a border war in 1979.

For its victims, communism could be much like Nazism. Only the language differed. Nazis spoke expressly of race. Communists concealed their racial motives behind talk of class and wealth. The victims did not differentiate.

Communists still conceal their racial motives. While Marxism lost the Cold War economically to capitalism with the collapse of the Soviet Union in 1991, it won the political conflict against a West still shaken by war and scarred by holocaust. We too became Europeans disillusioned with our races, cultures, and civilisation.

Our homeless West is a hybrid communist-capitalism predicated upon ideologies, without Western nations, races, or religion in play. More than just Marxists defeated the war-broken

West.

Communism and Nationalism

For Jews and the West, nations and cultures being communism's foe made nationalism communism's foe. Marxism opposed nationalism be it Western or Jewish.

For all the Marxist hostility to nationalism, the Soviet Union drew upon nationalism to inspire Russians to defend their Motherland from Germany during World War II. Nationalism worked, as communism did not, although communists subsequently denied any role for nationalism in the Soviet Union's defence. Because the Motherland was communist, they could characterise her defence as a defence of communism, not a defence of the Motherland.

When Ukrainians sided with Germans, it was because the Soviet Union was not their Motherland. Ukraine was their Motherland.

Nationalism also inspired the free West to defend our races and nations from Germany. We too would later downplay that inspiration. Because Nazi Germany was fascist, we could characterise our defence as a defence from fascism, not a defence of our Motherlands.

Not only do we dismiss the truth that our nationalism and racism saved us, we supersede the truth with the falsehood that we fought against nationalism and racism. Our retrospective World War II against Nazism is a retrospective war against everything in any way underlying the Holocaust, including Western nationalism, although Europeans other than Germans felt nationalism without harming Jews. So did most Germans.

Our redefined war against Western nationalism is a war against white people's self-respect, although Europeans other than Germans felt self-respect without harming Jews. So did most Germans.

The capitalism that prevailed at the end of the Cold War was a global capitalism, of the kind Hitler ascribed to Jews. Nationalist capitalism lost the Cold War as surely as communism lost, because Western nationalism lost. The West lost. Globalism won.

With the political victory of communism through the Cold War, we have come to accept, even admire, communist dictators while ostracising our democratically elected nationalists. When Europeans take up communism, they escape something of our racial guilt for the Holocaust with the ideological innocence accorded the opponents of Western nationalism: the opponents of Western races, cultures, and civilisations.

There is no ideological guilt. There is only racial guilt, for white people.

Among the ghoul galleries, Stalin and Mao wilfully killed many more people, but Hitler might well have been the single most destructive person in history. No idealists or ideologues were more brutal than communists, but killings by communists have not eaten away at equality, Marxism, or other ideology the way our revulsion at the Holocaust destroyed Western nationalism and racism.

Motive matters. We treat mass murder for apparently ideological reasons, which most massacres through the twentieth century claimed to be, as being less wrongful than killing Jews explicitly for their race.

The Unfinished War

Being told forever how wicked we used to be, our war against Nazis is a rare part of Western history in which we are free to feel pride. For all our talk of hating war, we have no problem with tens of millions of Europeans dying to defeat Nazism, now that we are not among them.

Not just our warriors fought. Night after night, Londoners braved the Blitz.

When the Holocaust superseded the rest of World War II to redefine that war and the rest of Western history, World War II became the West's unfinished war, but no longer do we fight the war from the viewpoint of our forebears. We fight it from the viewpoint of Jewry. We are uninterested in communist atrocities and other state-sanctioned killers enjoy partial or complete amnesties, but vengeful Jews and we hunt down former Nazis until the end of their lives.

If those long lives have not passed, they soon will, but the West remains obsessed with Nazism and Hitler. Around our fixation is a frenzy of sensitivity. People otherwise reasoned and rational will find a stark scent of Hitler in nondescript dark shadows and erupt into fury.

Refusing to consider any real present-day threat, we are not free to fight other races and their religions and are too frightened to do so, but Nazis offer us mythical foes. In our endless war-footing, we are ready to fight Nazis knowing we will never meet them, not any official original Nazis anyway. Nazism is the creed we fight as if it can never be eradicated, long after we stopped fighting ideologies.

Anti-Fascism

The fear of communism that seemed so pressing through the 1920s and '30s does not wash with us snug in the future. We are fixated with fascists.

If fascism is any nationalist authoritarianism, then a myriad of fascist regimes have arisen around the world. If fascism encompasses racist democracies, there are more.

They do not concern us. We only imagine white people being fascists. We only equate Western nationalism and racism with fascism.

From the perspectives of our endless individualism, fascism has come to mean any structures of a Western society. We deem all manner of Western authorities to be fascists for denying us the freedom to do whatever we want to do, however perverse that wanting might be. The worst of those authorities, we deem to be Nazis.

Nazism never seems more harmless than to read and hear people describe others as Nazis for maintaining the most trivial of rules and restrictions. Our forebears did not fight World War II for the freedom to make grammatical errors.

Thus Marxists in their hostility to the West and Western cultures and civilisation can characterise themselves as simply anti-fascist, without troubling themselves with the rest of Marxist ideology. It is quite an ironic turnaround, given that the impetus and most consistent characteristic of fascism was its defence of the West and Western peoples from Marxism.

Without Marxism, predating fascism by seventy years, there would have been no fascism. Without communists in power and seeking power because of the Great War, threatening invasion and revolution across the world, there still would have been no fascism.

First and foremost, fascism was resistance to communism. Fascists were the most passionate anti-communists.

If we think we fought World War II against fascism and fascism is any remnant of Western societies, then we fought the redefined World War II against Western societies. When the West sides with so-called anti-fascists as if the rest of us are not anti-fascist, we do not simply side with the Marxists and other races who despise us. We fight the people most willing to defend us, who defended us through World War II: Western nationalists.

Britons and other free Europeans were so anti-fascist, as fascism originally was, in 1939 that we went to war against fascist Germany by going to war against Germany. The communist Soviet Union did not fight fascist Germany until fascist Germany attacked it. Yet our rewriting of history makes our forebears who died defeating Nazism by defeating Germany into Nazis and fascists, while the communists who divided Poland with the Nazis are revered for being supposedly anti-fascist.

Marxists were only anti-fascist as fascism has come to be known, because fascists defended the West from Marxism. Marxists are still hostile to the West.

Marxists call dissidents reactionary for resisting their view of what they call progress. For the most part, terms like Nazi, fascist, far right, or hard right have become just as useful. The progressive mass is certain those dissidents are pining for the past because it is so keen to erase our Western past. It will believe anything that erases us.

The Conflict of Multiculturalism

Sorely scarred by the Holocaust, the West gave Jews special accommodations after World War II. Soon enough, the favours we granted Jews we granted other races and their religions.

The more we granted, the more they expected. The more we granted.

Racial diversity does not simply break down a society. It is intended to do so.

The imposition onto the West of what came to be known as multiculturalism began as essentially a racial conflict between Jews and Europeans much like Marxism, except that religious and irreligious Jews alike wanted multiculturalism, even if they disagreed as to what multiculturalism meant. Religious Jews wanted to maintain their faith. Irreligious Jews could be content to erase Judaism along with Christianity. Disillusioned Europeans sided with multiculturalism.

Western imperialism was globalisation premised upon Western self-belief. Multiculturalism submerges globalisation in our lack of self-belief, along with post-Holocaust Jewry's hostility to the West.

Like Soviet communism, multiculturalism is totalitarianism without white racism or nationalism. We do not call it fascism.

Unlike Soviet communism, multiculturalism respects other races' racism and nationalism. Multiculturalism became a conflict between white people and all other races, with increasing numbers of disillusioned white people siding with other races against their own.

Different races together fighting white people and cultures have become the primary commonality we have been able to conjure amidst racial diversity. It might be the only commonality.

Much as it is from the perspectives of our individualism, from the perspectives of other races, fascism becomes any structures of a Western society. The Nazi swastika symbolises not simply everything the world sees as wrong with white people. It symbolises white people altogether.

Thus white people defending our races, nations, and cultures are called fascists, without needing the willingness to recourse to violence of the original fascists. Resisting multiculturalism or any other policy or ideology harming Western Civilisation becomes fascism.

Behind those policies and ideologies is likely to be racial conflict much like that behind Marxism, pitting disillusioned Europeans with other races against their own. Immigrants who would oppose gender ideology, globalism, or environmentalism infesting their races and homelands support them for a trusting West that refuses to recognise racial interests.

Communists become allied with black and other non-white nationalists against white people. So do we.

Locked in our continuing war against fascism, our allies become all other races. Asserting their races, nations, and cultures wherever they are, they too oppose our races, nations, and cultures.

Our enemies are not African, Arab, or Asian. Our enemies are

Western.

Yet, white people concerned about the changing places in which we live do not want to don jackboots and goose-step through Nuremberg, any more than Japanese maintaining their racial and cultural integrity are about to invade Manchuria. We are so quick to describe white racists and nationalists as fascists, we do not imagine we are driving them to sympathise with fascism. We are certain they already do. If they are not wholeheartedly embracing other races and cultures, sacrificing their own, we call them fascists. We know how to deal with fascists.

When people accuse white people of bigotry, white supremacy, and fascism for expressing the same sentiments that remain unchallenged, even respected, among other races, they are attacking white people. It is a conflict against self-respecting white people, in which disillusioned white people side with other races against their own.

We refuse to fight other races or religions. Fighting fascism, we keep waging World War II against our own. Fascism comes to mean any Western resistance to our demise.

Our Fallen

We do not question World War II because we are taught it was a war against prejudice, but it was not at the time. Save only for the communist Soviet Union seeking to erase races and cultures altogether, racial and religious discrimination were the norm the world over, before and during the war. They still are.

Western soldiers, sailors, and airmen dead in ancient wars might have died for motivations we believe obsolete, but they died for something: their comrades beside them; their wives, children, and grandchildren; their generations unborn. Our nationalist dead died for their countries, when their countries were their races. The two were synonymous. White people died by the millions for Patria. They died for us.

Few people from other races fought in our armies, although it has become fashionable to speak of them out of all proportion to their numbers. Other races enjoying the benefits of our countries did not make our countries any less our countries, not then.

Without racism and other biological connectedness, we have

lost all sense of our war dead being of our race. Other races have not. When they desecrate our memorials, they know who they defile. They defile our forebears, not theirs. They defile us.

War memorials that speak of our soldiers dying for freedom do not speak of freedom in abstract. They died for their people's freedom.

The freedom for which we once fought wars was our freedom, not other people's freedom, along with a conviction we brought freedom and civilisation to other races. Freedom was intrinsic to having a country; enjoying one presumed enjoying the other, when we had nationalism and other collective identities.

Men and women dead in their country's name cannot have died to let their country disappear, but to bequeath their country to us and our descendants. They died in our defence.

If we wanted to honour our dead and wounded, we too would defend our countries, races, and Europe. There would be no mass immigration, multiculturalism, or globalism.

They who saw their comrades die did not surrender their senses of race and nation. We did that. They defended their races, nations, and cultures to the death in war, for us to surrender them in peace.

Redefining our Fallen

Few things more readily symbolise the loss of our countries than the loss of our flags. That is the reason we lose them.

Before we had multiculturalism, we had people. Our flags represented the people for whom our soldiers fought and died. Being barred from flying our flags because of the offence they cause other races brings home that we are discarding the countries for which our forebears thought they fought.

Our forebears fought foreigners to defend and restore our national borders. We fight each other to ensure our borders are not restored.

People who never went to war demand to speak for people who did, and even for God. Those who were not there interpret past wars in the image of their ideals – what they want wars to be – as the people who fought those wars never did.

Our soldiers, sailors, and airmen wounded or killed do not come into it. We impute reasons for their sacrifice the dead never imagined. Our forebears died for whatever we want them to have died.

That freedom our forebears died to give us we corrupt. We maintain they fought for freedoms, but not our people's freedoms.

We are not interested in freedom of speech for the old soldiers who fought, when they convey the reasons they did. Those soldiers can no longer be relied upon to know the reasons they fought. Dying for their races would be racist, dying for their nations nationalistic. We have decided they fought for something else altogether.

We want our forebears to have fought World War II against prejudice, although we berate them whenever we are confronted with their prejudice. We insist they died for tolerance, but only white people's tolerance.

Thus, we think we honour our dead and wounded not by defending our countries, races, and Europe, but by defending other races from our countries, races, and Europe. We submit to mass immigration, multiculturalism, and globalism.

When we redefine the reasons our forebears went to war, we are doing more than rejecting their values and motivations. We are giving them our values and motivations, imposing upon them our states of mind, although few of us fight for our values and motivations. We do not put ourselves out for anything.

Redefining old wars as we have done with World War II will not be an issue for future generations looking back at ours. We simple citizens do not sign up to serve. We do not die for anything. We employ soldiers to die.

For the most part, all we do is wage abuse upon each other, thinking we are better than our forebears who fought. We seize upon every little question mark over each other's ideology: talk of defending our countries and ways of life at odds with our vision of a single world populace.

We think it is our right, but it is our capacity: a freedom we have, because our forebears fought and died. So they become the reasons they did, however much they would have hated what we are doing with their countries and ours.

Our forebears defended our countries to the death, but may well have refused to fight had they known that we would give those same countries away, with barely a whimper of resistance. They might not have died for descendants and races that would come to reject them.

Giving our countries away, erasing our races and cultures, we dishonour our dead. Our governments that called upon our forebears to die in our defence now call upon us to die in our surrender.

No other races so glibly redefine the reasons of those who fought and died for them as the West now does with those who fought and died for us. We never honour people by redefining them, but we have to redefine our forebears' motivations and sacrifices. If we do not redefine them, while we are giving up our countries, cultures, and races, then our boys and girls died for nothing in war.

ABOUT THE AUTHOR

Simon Lennon has travelled throughout Europe, America, Australasia, Asia, and the South Pacific, seeing how similar European peoples are to each other (wherever we live) and how different we of the West are to everyone else. He has university bachelor's degrees in science and law and university master's degrees in commerce and business. He is married with six children.

His non-fiction collection *The West* comprises the following sixteen books:

Mending the West
The Unnatural West: An Overview
The Tribeless West: An Overview
The Homeless West: An Overview
The Vanishing West: An Overview

Individualism
Western Individualism
The End of Natural Selection
The Need for Nations

Identity
People's Identity: Race and Racism
Of Whom We're Born: Race and Family
Biological Us: Gender and Sexuality

Nationalism
A Land to Belong: Nationalism
The Failure of Multiculturalism

Cultures
Reclaiming Western Cultures
Christendom Lost
Aiding Islam

He is also the author of another non-fiction book, two collections of short stories, and five novels.